THE REASON FOR SPORTS

A CHRISTIAN FANIFESTO

TED KLUCK

MOODY PUBLISHERS
CHICAGO

© 2009 by
TED KLUCK

Scripture taken from the *Holy Bible, New International Version*®. NIV®. Copyright © 1973, 1978, 1984 by International Bible Society. Used by permission of Zondervan. All rights reserved.

Published in association with the literary agency of Wolgemuth & Associates, Inc.

Editor: Jim Vincent
Interior Design: Smartt Guys design
Cover Design: DogEared Design
Cover Image: Superstock

Library of Congress Cataloging-in-Publication Data

Kluck, Ted.
    The reason for sports : a Christian fanifesto / Ted Kluck.
    p. cm.
    Includes bibliographical references.
    ISBN 978-0-8024-5836-0
    1. Sports--Religious aspects. I. Title.

GV706.K57 209
205'.65--dc22

                          2009019622

This book is printed on acid free recycled paper containing 30% PCW (Post Consumer Waste) and manufactured in the United States of America by Bethany Press.

We hope you enjoy this book from Moody Publishers. Our goal is to provide high-quality, thought-provoking books and products that connect truth to your real needs and challenges. For more information on other books and products written and produced from a biblical perspective, go to www. moodypublishers.com or write to:

Moody Publishers
820 N. LaSalle Boulevard
Chicago, IL 60610

1 3 5 7 9 10 8 6 4 2

Printed in the United States of America

"This is not your normal sports book. Nor is it your normal Christian book. Here's to some abnormal reading then for those seeking a different point of view."
—Kenny Mayne
ESPN sports journalist

"Ted Kluck helps us think about sports Christianly without the Christian clichés and worn-out sports piety. He's an athlete and a fan whose writing implicitly reminds us why God created sports: for the joy of play."
—Mark Galli
Senior managing editor, *Christianity Today*

"Ted Kluck is passionate about sports. He's even more passionate about the gospel. You won't read any athletic rags-to-riches stories or find any cheesy quotes about 'leaving 100% on the field' in *The Reason for Sports*. Instead, you'll find insights into God, the gospel, and the sometimes crazy, sometimes wonderful world of sports."
—Stephen Altrogge
Author of *Game Day for the Glory of God*

"Ted makes it clear that while we do love our sports, the only real sports joy is found when honoring Jesus Christ. With much humor and much love, Ted gives enlightening and biting perspective on the athletes and events we remember most. What a treat to be convicted of our own idolotry of sports and, at the same time, laugh out loud! How can you not embrace a book that quotes both Allen Iverson and J. C. Ryle? Not a lot of sports guys reference 19th century evangelicals. (Ryle, that is . . . not Iverson.)"
—David Stein
Host, Sporting News Radio Network

"Most Christian books on sports are books about Christians playing sports. Not enough are books that give a Christian view on sports. This book fills the gap admirably. The writing is funny, honest, and provocative, and the subject matter is relentlessly interesting. Ted Kluck knows sports and knows how to write. We need more books like this one."
—Kevin DeYoung
Author of *Just Do Something*

For Ricky Williams, Mike Tyson,
and athletes everywhere.
I appreciate what you do.

CONTENTS

AUTHOR'S NOTE

BRIEF THOUGHTS ON THE USE OF THE WORD "FANIFESTO" IN THE TITLE

If you've read my book *Why We Love the Church*, or spend any time on my blog, *Ted Wins*, you know that I have a special hatred for the word "manifesto" when that word[1] is used in the subtitles of Christian books as it seems to be in about every other Christian book released these days. I'll be the first to admit that my dislike for this word isn't exactly rational. I mean, who hates a word? And for that matter, what's the big deal?

But you can imagine the sense of delicious irony I felt when the powers that be at Moody Publishing suggested using the word "fanifesto" as a part of the subtitle of my book. I remember where I was when I got the call (my office) and I remember having a hearty belly laugh over the irony. A guffaw. And then I considered my options. I could fight it, or I could just roll with it. I decided to roll with it on the condition that Moody wouldn't use any cheesy sports clip art or public-domain sports photography on the cover.

I learned a great deal through this little mini-negotiation. One, I learned that the word "essays" in the title of pretty much any project is usually the death-knell, sales wise, for that particular project. Still, that's what this book is. It's not a manifesto really . . . I imagine people who write manifestos tending to be the type of people who wear lots of drab olive garments and have posters of Che Guevara on their walls.

This really is just a collection of essays—but they're essays about why I love sports and why I love the gospel, and why I think you can (and should) love both of them together. And for the record, I like the word "fanifesto." I think it's clever.

NOTE

1. Other words I hate include "revolutionary."

INTRODUCTION

AUTOGRAPHS, CLICHÉS, *and the* SUMMER *of* MY DISCONTENT

I have a confession to make.

In the summer of 1994 I worked as a ball boy for the Indianapolis Colts. I had just graduated from high school and was myself a college football recruit of some (little) consequence.[1] Unbeknownst to me at the time, I wasn't good enough to make any real ripples in the sport, but I was just good enough to be obsessed about playing professional football and convinced myself that this was a possibility because I was as big as some of the Colts themselves (though they were infinitely faster, more agile, and more athletically touched by God). I was a hard worker. I was an overacheiver. Gritty. A hustler. I would make it, I thought. And besides, I was a good Christian[2] and God rewarded good, hardworking Christian athletes with lucrative contracts and "platforms" in pro sports, so that they could share the gospel.

Being around the Colts every day at their Anderson, Indiana, training camp was like cocaine for me. I got to lift with them in the weight
room—breaking the little ammonia caplets and inhaling just before
hoisting a heavy bar off my chest, just like the pros. I got to eat filet
mignon and swordfish with them in the cafeteria, and play Sega NBA
Jams (remember, this was 1994) tournaments with them in the dormitory at night. I got to launder their bright blue jerseys and affix the blue
horseshoe logo onto their helmets. I also got to refuse future NFL Hall
of Famer Marshall Faulk a ride after practice to the locker room in a
golf cart, after being told that I would be fired for doing so.[3] After the
last practice of the day, after all of the fans had left, I would strap on
my own cleats and go down to the immaculately manicured (think fair-
way-groomed) practice fields to hit their tackling dummies and run
through their agility ropes in my official "Property of Indianapolis
Colts" T-shirt.

One night, walking back through the empty parking lot toward the
dormitory where I stayed with the players, a car circled into the lot and
pulled up, idling slowly beside me. The car had two girls in it. They
weren't super-hot NFL groupie types, though I had learned, through
the summer, to spot these women. They looked very ordinary. Even a
little nervous. They looked like the kind of girls who probably graduated from Anderson High a few years ago and now looked forward to
hanging around training camp each summer for a little glimpse of fame.

They rolled down their window, and I figured they were going to
ask me for directions, or ask me what time practice started, or if I could
introduce them to Jim Harbaugh.[4] Instead, they asked me something
that has sort of haunted me ever since. They asked me for my autograph, thinking I was a real, live Indianapolis Colt and they had just
gotten lucky enough to catch me walking across the lot, unencumbered
by security.

I paused for a moment and ran through my options. I could tell them the long story about how, yes, I was a football player, but not for the Colts, and that my real job that summer was picking up dirty equipment and dragging blocking dummies on and off the practice field several times per day. But I figured that this would be met with confused looks, given my sweaty "Property of Indianapolis Colts" workout gear and reasonably athletic figure.

My heart pounded. The little egomaniac inside me had, for years, dreamed of signing autographs. I had dreamed of coming off the field and being unabashedly adored by children, young doe-eyed women, old matronly women, young men who wanted to be me, and older, cynical men who I had just won over emotionally by the strength of my game-winning performance. This was an empty parking lot in Anderson, Indiana, but I won't lie, it kind of felt similar.

I grabbed the paper and signed my name. Just like that. They smiled, thanked me, and drove away. Now they'll have a story to tell while working third shift, stocking shelves at Kroger. "We were driving around campus and met a Colts player," they'll say, giggling. They'll look at my name and wonder why it hasn't appeared on any rosters. They'll watch CBS Sports, expectantly, waiting to see my face on national television.

It's August 2008, or, rather, the Summer of Brett Favre. Favre, a Green Bay Packer legend, lock for the Hall of Fame, and all-around great American, has decided to retire and then unretire, making for a constant barrage of retrospectives, interviews, and speculation as to where he will end up. Even the fax machine upon which he transmitted his letter of reinstatement has become something of a celebrity. The Packers have made it clear that they are moving on without Favre, having drafted two high-profile quarterbacks[5] in recent drafts, and Favre has made it clear that Green Bay needs to welcome him back with open arms as the starter.

In doing so, Favre has unwittingly painted himself as the Typical Pro Athlete.[6] Obstinant. Egomaniacal. Concerned only with self. And for all of his supposed Midwestern, "old school," lantern-jawed Wrangler-wearing heroics, Favre is acting a lot like, well, Terrell Owens. This is sad, and is just one reason why I'm considering quitting sports entirely.

I'm also sick, it seems, of Christian athletes.

Christian sports writing, historically, has been cringe-worthy at best. A publisher puts out a title lauding the spiritual life of Christian Jock, and then crosses fingers, hoping that Christian Jock doesn't end up in jail, in divorce court, or embroiled in a paternity suit. These books are usually of the "by (Christian Athlete) with (local sportswriter)" variety and include the obligatory tales of a hardscrabble upbringing (made to sound hardscrabble even if it isn't exactly, well, hardscrabble), the wild early years as a pro, the rededication of one's life to Christ, at which point the blessings (Super Bowl, trophy wife, new contract, etc.) start to flow.

These books are okay if the reader also happens to be a Super Bowl champion; they would be relatable, then, at least. They're also probably okay if you're twelve years old. Otherwise, they leave the reader a little empty. A little let down. As though the beauty and passion they see from the athlete on the field was somehow translated into a subpar two-hundred-pages-with-photo-section that reads more like a really long public relations bio.

To many, the term *Christian athlete* means kneeling in the end zone for a self-congratulatory show of prayer, or a finger raised to the sky after tossing a touchdown pass. To others, it means that God is like a lucky pair of socks or a nutritional supplement, invoked at the right time in order to make one bigger, faster, or stronger in the moment of competition.

So what do we do with sports? What do we do with the scandals, the outsized personalities, the glamour, and the worldliness? Typically, evangelicals pull back. It's what we do. When we get skittish about movies, we stop watching them, or we make our own (usually with dreadful results). When we get nervous about public schools, sometimes we pull out. When we get convicted about music, we might burn our CD collections or sell our secular music to friends.[7]

If I were emergent, I would call this book a "manifesto" on why Christians should stay engaged with sports. On why pulling out is the last thing we should do, and on why there is still beauty, truth, and redemption to be found in athletics. (Well, we settled on *fanifesto* in the subtitle instead [see "Author's Note"].)

Sports are a huge part of the lives of American men, including church men. Our churches have informal basketball, golf, and softball leagues. Guys talk about sports in the church lobby. Yet with all the books teaching us how to worship with our marriages, our money, our "quiet times," and our sex lives, little is written about the subject that drives most of our banter with each other and around which much of our free time revolves. Sports.

How do we worship God with this part of our lives? How do sports help us to grow in sanctification? How do we think theologically about the myriad of moral dilemmas[8] in sports?

The last thing I want to do is to put out a book that subtly "ruins" sports for Christian guys, or that somehow equates loving sports to viewing porn.[9] I don't want Christian guys to hang their heads in shame because they spend more time watching (and enjoying) sports than they spend reading Bible stories to their toddler or asking their spouse about her day. But my hope is that Christians would begin to develop a theology of sports.

My own theology of sports has developed over a number of years as an athlete, and then several more years as a writer. Ironically, sports provides a lot of waiting around time—as anyone who has ever played or covered baseball can attest. There are lots of "Is this all there is?" moments spent sitting at press tables or waiting for press conferences to begin and end.

As Christians we tend to tackle topics like this with a grim determination. We clench our teeth and try to "unpack" sports. But the reason we care about sports at all is because they're fun. They're games. When we're done playing them we miss the inside jokes in the locker room. We miss making fun of our coaches. We miss the camaraderie. As fans we experience the rush of competition by watching athletes who are truly gifted by God, and we enjoy the bond we feel with other fans. On the pages that follow, hopefully, you'll be able to enjoy sports with me as I try to find the good in a sports world that at times has gone bad. I'm not going to try to convince you that Mike Tyson or Ricky Williams should be your spiritual guide, or that you shouldn't cheer for Mike Vick because he drowns puppies, or that you should cheer for all American QB Tim Tebow because he etches a Bible verse on his eyeblack before every game. I'll let you draw your own conclusions about all of those people. But I'll invite you to begin formulating your own theology of sports with me.

It would be twelve years before I would sign another autograph. It happened in 2006 when I played professional indoor football for the Battle Creek, Michigan, Crunch. (Now the defunct Crunch.) I had played only a year of college football before a couple of broken legs ended that dream, and then had bounced around no-pay "semipro" leagues ever since, suiting up for such notables as the Jackson Bombers (defunct), the Lansing Lightning (defunct), and the Delaware County Thunder (also defunct). Then I got to play for pay with the Continental Indoor Football League. While the CIFL wasn't exactly the big time,[10] it did offer me the opportunity to wear the Battle Creek Crunch uniform, run out of the tunnel, and sign autographs on the field after the game. I would soon come to realize that these autograph sessions were more about us, the players, than the fans. The autographs weren't worth the paper they were scribbled on. None of us were going anywhere, athletically. We were has-beens. Washed up.

Thanks to the CIFL and the BLT (the Bombers, Lightning, and Thunder), I had finally forgiven God for taking away my college football career. I had finally stopped wanting it. And I was even able to thank Him for taking it away because in its place was Him. He was bigger than my identity as an athlete. He allowed me to enjoy sports "compartmentally," which is how, I think, sports should be enjoyed, consumed, and thought about. By *compartmentally* I mean as a part of our greater whole, which should include sanctification and holiness in Him, something I certainly haven't mastered but to which I'm completely committed.

NOTES

1. Lots of letters from small to midsized colleges, saying things like "We'd really love to have you in our program." These were, of course, form letters.

2. Church on Sunday mornings and evenings, youth group, etc.

3. Faulk didn't want to lift weights, and also didn't want to be bothered by the task of walking through throngs of adoring fans all clamoring for his autograph. As it turns out he really didn't need to lift the weights, and ended up being one of the most effective dual-threat running backs in NFL history. I remember, that summer, feeling like Faulk was the fastest runner from a dead stop to full speed that I had ever seen in my life. Faulk was one of the few players—I would also put Walter Payton and to a certain extent Eric Dickerson in this category though in a more one dimensional way—who elevated carrying the football to an art form. He made it look effortless and artful, as opposed to just huge guys crashing into each other.

4. Besides Faulk, Harbaugh was the closest thing the Colts had to an actual, bankable star that summer. He was a stud in the Big Ten at the University of Michigan, and had done reasonably well as the quarterback of the Chicago Bears in previous years. Also, writers are always talking about how so-and-so had "matinee-idol" good looks. Harbaugh actually had them. He actually had a "lantern jaw."

5. Brian Brohm and Aaron Rodgers, who should get some kind of an award for putting up with Favre's "I think I'm going to retire only to return" song and dance pretty much every year during his final five seasons with Green Bay.

6. There are a lot of other holdouts this summer, including my fantasy running back Steven Jackson, another rags-to-apparently-not-enough riches story in Packers running back Ryan Grant, and Bills Pro Bowl offensive tackle Jason Peters.

7. Note: This was a great way to score cheap, excellent rock albums at Taylor University, where I went to school. This usually happened after a particularly convicting "secular music is bad" chapel service.

8. What would John Calvin say about Michael Vick drowning pit bulls, trainer Brian McNamee allegedly injecting Roger Clemens *and* Clemens's wife, Nick Saban lying . . . or Mike Tyson being Mike Tyson?

9. "Hey, this is your sports accountability partner speaking. How many ESPN.com highlights did you watch today? Are you looking at sports right now?"

10. There's one party scene in *Major League* where a woman asks the Tom Berenger character if pro ballplayers get paid a lot, and he responds, "It depends on how good you are." The woman then asks, "How good are you?" to which Berenger responds, "I make the league minimum." I made the league minimum in the CIFL, which amounted to $150 per game.

1

IT'S HARD *to* SAY
I'M SORRY

SIN, CONFESSION,
AND THE JOCK APOLOGY

*I say, furthermore, that "a sin," to speak more particularly, consists
in doing, saying, thinking, or imagining anything which is not in
perfect conformity with the mind and law of God.*

J. C. RYLE
Holiness

My son watches a lot of sports because I watch a lot of sports. He's
five, and he's giggled at beer commercials (he likes the Coors
Silver Bullet train) and not (thankfully) asked me to define "erectile dysfunction" when forced to sit through commercials that portray old men
either singing about Viagra in a deserted roadside bar or, inexplicably,
two people sitting outside in different bathtubs, watching a sunset. He's
also watched an unhealthy amount of jock press conferences. He
knows the phrase "it is what it is." And as such, he's sat through an inordinate amount of jock apologies.

These are, for the uninitiated, apologies by people (athletes) who
don't really apologize. They're apologies that were written by twenty-
one-year-old interns in the PR department. They usually say things
like, "I'm sorry if anyone was hurt by what I said." Translation: You're

too sensitive. Or, "We just need to put this behind us and move on." Translation: I'd like to move on as soon as possible, if only you could let me forget that I took money from a booster, used steroids, ran over an old lady with my car, or shoved a fan who trashed my mom.

In sports, as in postmodern society, the idea that there is sin (and therefore true repentance) is ludicrous. Athletes apologize because they have to. They apologize because they've been caught. Luis Castillo, who is by all accounts a great guy, got caught for taking steroids to heal an injury before the NFL combine, where scouts and executives check out athletes before the NFL draft. He apologized afterward, essentially for getting caught, sending a letter to each and every NFL club, "apologizing" for his "mistake." He was still drafted in the first round and is a millionaire today. In sports, repentance means being acquitted or having the charges dropped.

Below are a couple of years' worth of real jock apologies I compiled in the early 2000s from a variety of college and pro sports. What they all have in common is a complete inability to actually apologize for what they've done wrong. Afterward, you'll find a Jock Apology Generator in which you pull sentences from each of the three scenarios to craft your own, PR-friendly, athlete apology.[1] You can learn a lot about how *not* to take responsibility by reading these varied ways of "Please excuse me from the consequences and let me get on with my life" apologies.

The Kellen Winslow Method, Part One:
Expressing Regret (but Not Repentance)

Team: University of Miami   **Position:** tight end

The Incident: A postgame rant

The Apology: "After speaking with the press, I immediately regretted my comments and felt embarrassed for my family, my team, the University of Miami, our fans, alumni, and myself."

How It Works: It's critical to express embarrassment on behalf of your team, company, wife, kids, aunt, uncle, dry cleaner. Tears are helpful as well, but not required.

The Kellen Winslow Method, Part Two: The Learning Experience

The Apology: "What I have learned from this experience is to take my triumphs and failures in stride. My outburst should in no shape or form be a reflection on this institution or the Miami football program."

How It Works: Try to express the fact that every irresponsible and damaging thing you've ever done is simply a learning experience, like homework. And most importantly, you'll need to absolve your employer (in this case, Miami football) of any responsibility for your embarrassing actions.

The Jeremy Shockey Method: The Blanket Pseudoapology

Team: New York Giants   **Position:** tight end

The Incident: A homosexual slur

The Apology: "I guess I do regret saying it. I didn't think anyone was going to make a big deal out of it. I'm not prejudiced against anybody's beliefs or what they do in their off time. I do regret saying something like that. Whatever I did to offend people, I apologize."

How It Works: The blanket pseudoapology gets you off the public hook without actually making a pride-killing apology. Also, the blanket "whatever I did to offend anybody" statement clears you of any further responsibility.

21

The Mike Price Method:
Expressing Admiration Apology

Team: University of Alabama (sort of)   **Position:** head coach (just through one spring football practice)

The Incident: Being intoxicated and visiting an exotic dancer

The Apology: "Over the past several days, I have been saddened by the rumors that have been swirling about my conduct. I have had numerous truthful and honest discussions with the president and our athletic director, Mal Moore—our fine athletic director, Mal Moore, who has dedicated many, many years of service to this university and I was proud to have been picked by him."

How It Works: The key here is to gratuitously compliment the people who hold your job in their hands. Also, it is important to shift the blame to everyone else by expressing "sadness" over the rumors that you helped create.

The Rasheed Wallace/Damon Stoudamire Method:
The Coach Apology

Team: Portland Trail Blazers   **Position:** forward, guard, respectively

The Incident: Arrested for possession of marijuana

The Apology: "They're deeply sorry for what happened, as we all are."

How It Works: Why apologize yourself when you can get your coach (in this case, Maurice Cheeks), who likely makes a pittance compared to you, to do it for you?

The Pete Rose Method:
The Nonapology

Team: Cincinnati Reds   **Position:** second baseman

The Incident: Accused of betting on Reds baseball games; later banned from Major League Baseball "for conduct detrimental to baseball"

The Apology: "No, no, Jim, not at all. I'm not going to admit to something that didn't happen. I know you get tired of hearing me say that, but I appreciate the ovation. I appreciate the American fans voting me on that all-century team. I'm just a small part of a big deal tonight."

How It Works: Rose uses a technique that we like to call "not apologizing at all." And then he takes special care to turn the conversation back around to the love we all feel for him. This method might keep you out of baseball, but it will land you plenty of opportunities to sit at card shows in cities like Bettendorf, Iowa, where you can sign your autograph.

The Chris McAlister Method:
The Ongoing Apology

Team: Baltimore Ravens   **Position:** cornerback

The Incident: Violating team rules during a road game

The Apology: "I've already apologized and am still apologizing to a lot of my teammates for what happened last weekend. [Coach] Billick hit it this weekend, he hit it [yesterday] with the media, and my teammates have talked about it. It's something that we're moving forward, going past."

How It Works: When in doubt, keep apologizing. And talk about how important it is to "move forward" and "put this behind you."

The Allen Iverson Method:
The Legalese/Promotional Apology

Team: Philadelphia 76ers   **Position:** guard

The Incident: Homophobic slurs in rap album

The Apology: "If individuals of the gay community and women of the world are offended by any of the material in my upcoming album, let the record show that I wish to extend a profound apology."

How It Works: While apologizing, take special care to mention your upcoming album, book, or movie. Make the media work for you. And remember, going on record now saves a lot of heartache later.

The "It Is What It Is"
Jock Apology Generator

How It Works: ". . . and you'll find a nice buffet available in the press room at no charge." Best to add tears to this apology.

Instructions: Using one phrase from each group listed below, craft your own professional athlete apology for personal use.

Group 1:

- I would like to apologize first and foremost to my fans.
- I would like to apologize to my teammates and absolve my team of any responsibility.
- I would like to apologize to alumni of this fine institution of higher learning.
- I would like to apologize to my family.

Group 2:

- The drugs were not mine, but I still take full responsibility for my actions.
- It was not my intention to physically assault _____.
- I truly do not know how the roughly $15,000 of stereo equipment got into my vehicle.

Group 3:

- The most important thing now is to put this issue behind us.
- We need to move forward as a team, starting right now.
- It's now time to focus on winning.

Here's an example of the jock apology generator in action: "I would like to apologize first and foremost to my fans. The drugs were not mine, but I still take full responsibility for my actions. The most important thing now is to put this issue behind us."

Believe me when I write that I don't expect athletes to be perfect. I am far from perfect myself, and thank God that there weren't people following me with cameras and notebooks in my early twenties, looking to record my every thought, action, and idea for posterity. God's grace is big and sufficient. But that said, athletes, especially Christian athletes, should try to model true, biblical repentance when put in a public apology situation because it's a way to honor God and grow in sanctification.

J. C. Ryle writes that a mark of "growth in grace" is increased humility. So where is the athlete who has the courage to say, with Job, "I am vile" or with Peter, "I am a sinful man, O Lord"? Where is the athlete willing to ask the forgiveness of God, in front of a nation of fans and press?

In 2008 Tiger Woods, largely recognized as the greatest golfer and endorser of Buick products to have ever walked the earth, was on his way to doing the undoable: winning every golf tournament he entered in a given year. Woods is also almost universally accepted, in that Michael Jordanian way, as an all-around swell guy—a friend of Madison Avenue and sports fans alike. Parents hold him up as an example of hard work, and as a golfer who isn't a professional just because he grew up a child of privilege like most golfers do. Woods, it is understood, is also wildly competitive, single-minded, and driven as are most successful pro athletes.

TIGER, TIGER, BURNING BRIGHT

Woods's pursuit of a perfect season ended on March 24 in Miami, when he finished two shots back of Geoff Ogilvy, but it was on the final hole of the tournament that Woods unleashed a stream of invectives at a photographer who dared to snap his shutter during the golfer's backswing. He went so far as to threaten to break the neck of the next photographer who dared to do the same thing.

Now, far be it from me to preach restraint in the heat of battle, as I am perhaps the sorest loser to have walked the face of the earth. I've thought, and said, things I've regretted in the heat of battle and thank God for the fact that those things have never made it to print. I have wanted to find opponents in the parking lot after games—and not to share the four spiritual laws with them, if you know what I mean.

But after the round, rather than apologize or take responsibility for his actions, Woods offered the following: "Each time it's happened, well, three out of four times, I made bogey," he said of midswing camera clicks. "You have no idea what's been said on the golf course all the time, in any sport really. It was the heat of the moment."

So let this be a word of caution to fans and the media who dare to snap a shutter, clear their throat, or draw a breath when a professional golfer is in his backswing. Like Tiger, he may try to break your neck and may not be sorry about that either.

Tiger's rant and lack of remorse for his escapade is also an interesting perspective on sin and confession, and how it just doesn't seem to exist in sports. The fact of the matter is that the heat of the battle is precisely when our true character is revealed.

Woods could have said, "It was wrong for me to say what I said to the photographer. I really regret that and am embarrassed by it. I'll do my best to see that nothing like that ever happens again." Instead what he said, in effect, was, "What I said really wasn't that bad, as compared to the really nasty stuff that gets said behind the scenes," and "I could have gotten a bogey, which makes what I did completely justifiable."

If he'd really apologized, fans and the media would have been impressed by Woods's humility, the photographer would have had public closure to his mistake, and the kids watching at home (Are there kids watching golf at home? Do kids buy Buicks?) would have seen a real, live example of confession and repentance in action.

The case of Olympic uber-swimmer Michael Phelps is interesting as well. Months after shattering Olympic records and taking home a truckload of gold medals, Phelps was photographed inhaling from a marijuana pipe. Phelps, at the time, was already a pitchman for everything from cell phones to cereal. He was tailor-made for Madison Avenue in that he was young, white, humble, and on television a lot.

As is the case with many professional athletes, we made the same mistake that Madison Avenue made, in that we put our hope and trust in a young man who, as far as we could tell, had the ability to jump in the pool and swim faster than anybody on the planet. In that regard he was stellar. In essence, advertisers were saying, "Because Michael Phelps can jump in a pool and swim faster than other people, you should buy our product." This is a gamble advertisers make all the time. Unfortunately, lots of other people, kids included, made that emotional gamble as well.

His Olympic performances made us cheer, and they're no less worthy of our cheers now. Phelps did apologize for his actions, and his apology expressed true regret:

"I engaged in behavior which was regrettable and demonstrated bad judgment," Phelps said. "I'm twenty-three years old and despite

the successes I've had in the pool, I acted in a youthful and inappro-
priate way, not in a manner people have come to expect from me. For
this, I am sorry. I promise my fans and the public it will not happen
again."

His case suggests that perhaps as fans, parents, and writers, we
should guard our hearts a little more closely when it comes to choosing
heroes for our kids and our readers. Of course, the Phelps story is not
yet over, and he may still be capable of great moral and athletic success
as time passes.

We can hear crying from the basement, getting increasingly louder
as Ian, the pastor's four-year-old son, makes his way up the stairs. As
any parents of young children know, these meltdowns happen on a regular basis when your family spends time with another family. The conversation is put on hold, the fire is put out, and you try to resume
talking where you left off.

Except this time, when Ian rounded the corner, it looked like he'd
lost a fight with NHL enforcer Mike Ricci. His face was a bloody mess
of red, and he was gushing from his little round four-year-old nose. Between gasping cries, he sputtered out the name of my son, Tristan, who
I knew was responsible before Ian rounded the corner. To say that
these kids "play rough" would be an understatement. That would be
like saying that NHL tough guy Tie Domi played rough on the ice in
the mid-1990s. When Tris and Ian play together, it's clash of the titans.

Tristan rounded the corner a moment later, looking sheepish. He
knew that he was wrong, and that while he hadn't intended to bash his
little friend in the nose, it happened. If he had been a professional athlete, his agent would have crafted a statement to this effect: "I regret
that Ian's face collided with a ball that I threw. Sometimes basement
play can get rough, and I have no control over that aspect of it. I give my

best to Ian and his family in hopes that we can all move past this and put this unfortunate incident behind us."

Gladly, Tristan isn't a pro athlete. He's five and he still knows how to apologize. His heart isn't so hardened, and he's not so jaded by things like public relations and spin, that he can still manage to be genuinely contrite about things. I pray that this will be the case when he's twenty-five and apologizing to his spouse for something, or (God forbid) apologizing on national television for something he did as a high-profile athlete.

The cross and the gospel are, by nature, offensive. It's off-putting to suggest that sin exists in a world that tries so hard, like Woods and all of the jock apologizers, to justify it. As athletes, we want to thank God for our touchdowns, write "all things possible" in marker on our wrist tape or shoes, and kneel in the end zone after we score. But that's only half the story. We want to live like Jesus. Give talks. Maybe even start nonprofit foundations. But perhaps the most Christian thing we could do, from the stage, is acknowledge our own sin. And as fans, we need to realize our role models are human, sinners just like us, and extend the grace to forgive when they sin and act for their own self-interests. Perhaps the most Christian thing we can do is to pray for their ministry with other athletes and their walk with Christ.

NOTE

1. Adapted from Ted Kluck, "How to Apologize Like a Pro," ESPN.com, Page 2, at http://espn.go.com/page2/s/kluck/031112.html. Reprinted with permission of ESPN.com, Page 2.

2

WILDER *at* HEART

STEROIDS, HGH, AND
BUILDING THE BIGGER ATHLETE

*If me and King Kong went into an alley, only one of us would come
out. And it wouldn't be the monkey.*

LYLE ALZADO
Oakland (Los Angeles) Raiders

A confession: I've always wanted to use steroids.

Starting in early high school and continuing through college,
any time I had to come up with an MLA research paper, I would do
these papers on anabolic steroids, human growth hormone, an-
drostenedione, or some other such performance enhancing drug (here-
after referred to as PED for simplicity's sake).

In early high school my build could best be described as "lanky."
And as any body-image-obsessed, pasty-skinned, socially awkward
adolescent boy will attest, lanky is not really what you're shooting for
in high school. "Well-muscled, ripped, or King of the Jungle" would be
more along acceptable lines. Kicking sand in the face of the bully on
the beach. Girls asking to feel your muscles in the hallway. These are
the things about which (some) young male high school athletes dream.

So I'd take the books from the library and research the steroids. Then I bought and cited the bodybuilding magazines—and the result, I'm sure, was a handful of staggeringly cruddy papers. I would tick off the litany of side effects—short temper, testicular atrophy (giggles from classmates), heart problems, liver problems, emotional problems (anger, fits of rage)—and then the desired results—staggering increases in muscle mass, decreases in body fat, improved speed. And while my classmates were experimenting with their first joint or heavier recreational drugs, I was learning about the only drug that ever tempted me—the muscle building, speed increasing PED.

Finally I saved money and decided to buy "nutritional" supplements at health-food stores. These supplements weren't regulated by the FDA, as they were neither "food" nor "drugs." They went by names like "Rocket Fuel" and "Animal Pack," the latter of which was a smattering of huge pills that came in daily, shrink-wrapped portions and turned my urine a disturbingly neon shade of yellow/green and may have done other things to my body as well. I knew they weren't steroids, but honestly I hoped they would provide similar results.

Lyle Alzado, a defensive lineman for the Denver Broncos, the Cleveland Browns, and, most famously, the Raiders, died in 1992, which was the end of my sophomore year of high school. He was forty-three years old and died of a brain tumor, which he asserted was brought about by his copious steroid use that started in 1969 (college, for him) and never ended. He claimed to be mentally addicted to the drugs, and once claimed that there wasn't a man on earth whose [behind] he couldn't kick, which I'm sure wasn't technically true but must still be a great feeling. Toward the end of his career he admitted to using natural human growth hormone (harvested from cadavers) in order to gain an edge on the field and fuel a comeback in 1990 that would ultimately be ill-fated.

All of this was documented in a *Sports Illustrated* article whose cover portrayed a cancer-ridden Alzado wearing a do-rag around his head and imploring readers to not make the same mistake he did. What the article also did, however, was recount in breathy detail the unhuman gains in weight, strength, and speed that Alzado experienced while on the drug that, at age fifteen, I spent most of my time thinking about.

It should be noted here that in my years as an athlete/writer/person-hanging-around-sports, I've pretty much decided that steroids do absolutely work. They will make a slow man faster. They will make a fast man really fast. Ditto with strength. But I've also decided that you have to be a pretty unbelievable athlete to begin with, to have steroids make any impact whatsoever on taking you to the "next level." Lyle Alzado was discovered playing college football at Yankton College (South Dakota)[1] and drafted in the fourth round by the Denver Broncos because he was a really good football player.

By contrast, I played small college football with a handful of guys who were decent players, and became more decent by using steroids. But their more decentness was probably only noticed and appreciated by those few of us on the "inside" of the program. I also played with washed-up semipro players who were markedly stronger but still every bit as washed-up and futureless while spending lots of cash and sacrificing their health on black market PEDs.

Here's a "short list" of athletes[2] who have tested positive for or admitted use of steroids or other performance enhancing drugs:

Lyle Alzado
Chris Cooper (the Raiders defensive lineman, not the Academy
　　　　　Award winning actor)
Tony Mandarich

Shawne Merriman

Ken Caminiti

Jose Canseco

Rafael Palmeiro

Andy Pettitte

Justin Gatlin (a sprinter)

Ben Johnson (another sprinter)

Tim Montgomery (another sprinter)

Marion Jones (yet another sprinter and a former Nike pitchwoman)

Floyd Landis (a cyclist)

Many others have been implicated or their names have appeared in the media in PED-related scandals over the past several years.

At the 2008 NFL Scouting Combine,[3] a player named Quentin Groves stuck his hand into the amazingly grasslike FieldTurf and rocketed out of his stance while hundreds of team-gear-clad NFL coaches and scout types clicked their stopwatches in unison. FieldTurf is known as a fast surface, and this 40-yard sprint had the potential to make or lose a lot of money for Quentin Groves and the other young men like him who were milling around at the starting line waiting to run their own 40-yard dashes.

If Groves is anything like his counterparts, he probably began training for this event a few hours after the completion of his last college game. He signed with an agent, and was whisked to one of the many "speed schools" or athletic performance academies that have popped up all over the country where he spent most of his waking hours training for this event, eating so that he can be leaner for this event, and lifting so that he can be stronger for this event. He covers the distance in 4.57 seconds, which is most notable because Groves weighs 250 pounds and plays defensive end. By way of comparison, Jerry Rice (weight: around 195), widely considered the greatest wide receiver in NFL history, ran a 4.7 second 40-yard dash, and Emmitt Smith (weight: 210), the NFL's all-time leading rusher, ran in the 4.8 neighborhood.

This is in no way meant to insinuate that Groves takes or has ever taken steroids; it's only meant to insinuate that something has clearly changed in training/nutrition/etc. since Jerry Rice ran his very-pedestrian-but-still-fast 4.7. For what it's worth, Shawne Merriman (who has been suspended for PED-related transgressions—see list above) ran a 4.68 while at the same time weighing 272 pounds. He considered the time slow.

I'm not a physician, but it's not at all surprising that when bodies are that huge and move that fast, the result is a whole lot of concussions, torn ACLs, back spasms, high-ankle sprains, pulled groins, sprained AC joints, and, occasionally, broken necks. I'm not of the belief that God created our bodies to be that big and move that fast at the same time.

IT'S CALLED CHEATING

But sports and cheating have always been strange bedfellows. And let's, for the record, call PED use what it is: cheating. Sin, if you will. A willful attempt to subjugate the rules of the game for the furthering of one's own career. (So when Christian ballplayer Andy Pettitte halfway apologizes but asserts that he "doesn't consider himself a cheater" in 2008 for taking human growth hormone [HGH] to rehabilitate a shoulder injury, he is still a cheater. He just hasn't fully grasped it yet. He asserts that he "didn't do it to get an advantage," but isn't taking a banned substance to recover faster from a shoulder injury so that you can play baseball again exactly that?) Besides trying to gain an advantage, taking PEDs diminishes the key goal of sports: to treat fans to a fair competition in which skilled athletes achieve success with their natural abilities. The joy comes from human achievement, not medical enhancement.

The dollar amounts on the line for top performing athletes are huge. In 2007, second overall NFL draft choice Calvin Johnson received a six-year deal totaling $64 million—$27.2 million of it *guaranteed*, which is comparable to the gross domestic product of a small third world country. All that to say, there's a lot of money involved for kids who probably haven't seen a lot of money in their lives. It's the promise of untold fame and riches, and the ability to provide for one's children, grandchildren, and great-grandchildren. It's still cheating.

As I wrote in my *Sports Spectrum* magazine column, baseball has always had a fairly nebulous relationship with cheating—not just with PEDs but manipulation of sports equipment too, especially balls and bats. When a noodle-armed geezer like Gaylord Perry scuffs, spits-on, or otherwise alters the ball, he is remembered as simple folklore—as a sort of wink-wink, boys-will-be-boys part of the fabric of baseball.

However, when Barry Bonds (allegedly) jams a needle full of HGH into his backside, even hardened sportswriters call it cheating. And it is . . . but so is scuffing the ball, corking the bat (to increase bat speed), slathering the bat in pine tar, and all of the other things baseball apologists forgive on a pretty regular basis.

So should Mark McGwire, Sammy Sosa, Bonds, and everybody else who mysteriously gained fifty pounds of rock-hard muscle and started blasting baseballs out of stadiums be kept out of the Hall of Fame? Probably, but my question is, how do you keep them out?

Is it sad that in my sons' generation baseball conversations will center around "Who's on the juice?" rather than "Who's your favorite player?" Of course, it's tragic.[4]

The Yankees' Alex Rodriguez (A-Rod to his friends) admitted recently that he used steroids as a member of the Texas Rangers, from 2001–2003, a period in which he hit 156 home runs. He made the admission after *Sports Illustrated* mentioned his name in conjunction with a 2003 steroid test—the results of which were supposed to be kept confidential and in which 104 players were named. This, after denying he'd ever taken performance-enhancing substances. Rodriguez attributed his drug use to a "loosey-goosey" clubhouse culture that condoned everything, provided results were being achieved.

There's no denying that Major League Baseball turned an opportunistic blind eye for too long. Rodriguez was right about the clubhouse culture. And he was, in a PR sense, savvy for admitting his drug use instead of cartoonishly denying it a la Bonds, Clemens, McGwire, Sosa, and Palmeiro—men who have all had their eternal legacies tarnished as much for their ridiculous denials as for the actual sin itself.

BECOMING AN ARMCHAIR CHEMIST

Many fans have become armchair chemists over the course of the last decade, deciding which lantern-jawed (and now, bull-foreheaded) baseball/football/cycling/track hero got to the top by saying his prayers and taking his vitamins, and which one got there by saying his prayers and visiting his neighborhood medicine man to grab the latest undetectable designer steroid.

After a crippling player strike, Major League Baseball was experiencing its death rattle in the late 1990s. So when baseballs started flying out of ballparks a couple years after the strike ended, MLB was all too happy to turn a blind eye and let Sosa, McGwire, and later Bonds revive the sport with their epic home run battles. The truth is the Sosa/McGwire race for the home run record was fun for everybody, myself included. They kick-started the nation's interest in baseball—but now the nation, and baseball, is paying the price. Keeping them out of the Hall of Fame would be embarrassing, but letting them in will be even more so. And it's just what Major League Baseball deserves.[5]

Baseball is a game built largely around the love of statistics—sitting in your bedroom, reading the backs of baseball cards by the light streaming in your windows from the mean streets of Grand Rapids. It's about knowing that despite your uncertainty about large issues like Calvinism vs. Arminianism or the will of God, at least you can recite Coco Crisp's batting average from 2003 (.266). It's about restoring order to chaos—not creating more chaos, as is the case with asterisked records, and the fact that Hank Aaron will have been lapped by two guys (Bonds and A-Rod) with less than pure blood flowing through their bulging veins.

Unfortunately, thanks to BALCO, the Mitchell Report, and the steroid era, our kids know almost as much about pharmaceuticals and legal proceedings as batting averages and on-base percentages. They'll know the duties of the House Oversight and Government Reform Committee before they'll be able to explain the infield fly rule. The real stars of this show are, of course, the attorneys.

Should baseball offer amnesty to all pre-Mitchell Report users of steroids and HGH and start over with tough testing? Amnesty means that the statistics still mean something. It means "forgive and forget." No asterisks and no omissions. It means that even though Mark McGwire (allegedly) had the combined testosterone level of Rambo, Arnold Schwarzenegger, and John *Wild at Heart* Eldredge flowing through his bulging veins, he still hit the ball out of the park seventy times. No small feat. But if we give amnesty to these juiced-up roid freaks, we'll have to grant the same to Pete Rose, who was as handy with the *Daily Racing Form* as Sammy Sosa was (allegedly) with the syringe.

As for tough testing, you read it here first: Equip all MLB clubhouse urinals with the technology to immediately detect elevated testosterone levels. In fact, do this for all urinals, everywhere, just to be safe. I want to know my accountant and favorite magazine columnists aren't hitting the needle on the way into the office. Hey, if we can put men on the moon, we can do this. In fact, we have to do this. The future of baseball depends on it.

And until then, kids, good luck reading the 311-page Mitchell Report each night, by the light streaming in your bedroom window.[6]

For the athlete, there's more to the appeal of steroids than potential financial payouts on the other side. It's the Alzado appeal. It's liking the idea that you could walk into the dark alley with King Kong and come out on top. And as sprinter Harold Abrahams said, famously, in *Chariots of Fire*: "I don't run to take beatings, I run to win." We play sports (and, for that matter, write and conduct business) so that we can be the guy who walks out of the alley. Unfortunately, running to win, today, seems to involve running to the pharmacy first.

But this speaks to a greater spiritual issue than just cheating, and just using steroids, because, let's face it, most Christian athletes probably aren't going to use steroids (though some surely have, and will). Rather, it speaks to where we find our identity. Do we, like Abrahams, find our identity solely in winning? And like Alzado, do we find it in being able to be the only man to walk out of the alley? We can ask ourselves this in light of sports, or business, or pickup games at the YMCA. Of course, we play to win, but we should be living to do more than win games. Even if those games have the potential to make us a lot of money.

I've never met an athlete who, at the end of their career, communicated something to the effect of "I really wish I'd used steroids so that I could have squeezed out another year or two," or "I'm really glad I used anabolic steroids or human growth hormone." Many don't talk about it at all, some express regret, or embarrassment at what to tell their kids. Some (see: Roger Clemens, Bonds, Pettitte, McGwire et al.) end up in court, thinking that by glad-handing some congressmen and signing a few baseballs[7] they'll be able to avoid judgment.

I often wonder what to tell my kid. He sees me lifting weights every couple of days in the basement but doesn't see me making the kind of gains he sees on Shawne Merriman every Sunday afternoon. He seems reasonably interested in sports, so sometime he'll have to deal with the fact that there's a pill out there that could turn him into a winner.[8] But it's a pill he can't use without breaking covenant with our Lord—a consequence far more grievous than testicular atrophy, back acne, or a short temper.

And as much as I love to win, I hate to lose more. With regard to sports, in many ways I identify deeply with Harold Abrahams—I loved winning just because it wasn't losing. I was a miserable athletic soul. I won to stave off losing. Hence, the unbelievable pull of these drugs.

But I want my son to know that if he is a godly loser I will respect him deeply. I pray that he won't be as shortsighted as his father, and he won't, even for a year or two, find his identity in games or bench presses or 40-yard dash times. And I want him to know that he is to work as unto the Lord and play to win, but if he loses, and loses with integrity, that it will be an honor to go into that alley, just to carry him out.

NOTES

1. Yankton, a small liberal arts college that was affiliated with the United Church of Christ, closed its doors in 1984.

2. Without using the now-famous report compiled by Senator George Mitchell.

3. The NFL Scouting Combine is an annual meeting of NFL scouts, coaches, front-office types, and team doctors that takes place behind closed doors in Indianapolis for the purpose of poking, prodding, X-raying, and otherwise evaluating some 250 of college football's most promising prospects. More on the combine in chapter 10.

4. The preceding material was adapted from the author's *Sports Spectrum* magazine column, "Pro and Con," *Sports Spectrum*, July/August 2007, 17.

5. Ibid.

6. Adapted from Ted Kluck, "Pro and Con," *Sports Spectrum*, May/June 2008, 18.

7. Shortly before he was called in to testify about his own steroid use, Roger Clemens took a goodwill tour through Capitol Hill, signing baseballs for starstruck, jock-sniffing politicians. This was one of the most arrogant things I think I've ever seen in sports. However, at press time it still doesn't look like it will be enough to exonerate The Rocket.

8. According to a survey by the Center for Disease Control and Prevention, steroid use among high school students more than doubled between 1991 and 2003. More than 6 percent of 15,000 students surveyed admitted trying steroid pills or injections. At the same time, less than 4 percent of the nation's high schools were testing for steroids, according to the National Federation of State High School Association's survey of athletic directors.

3

HONESTY (AUTHENTICITY) *and* SPORTS

WHY I LOVE MIKE TYSON AND RICKY WILLIAMS AND YOU SHOULD TOO

Sometimes I feel like everyone hates me.

MIKE TYSON
Boxer

everal years ago I stood on the roof of a hotel in Washington, D.C., with a cell phone glued to my ear talking about Mike Tyson. Nearby, at the rooftop pool, a Middle Eastern looking couple got out of the water on an unseasonably warm spring day—the kind of day that makes you want to buy a skateboard.

I felt important partly because I was writing a book on Mike Tyson, and partly because in a few hours I'd watch him fight in person for the first time. When a big fight[1] happens to a city, it's like a huge, adult circus coming to town. You start seeing strange things, like men wearing baseball jerseys and backward ball caps in very nice restaurants. You also see men wearing vests with no shirt underneath, and not because they're trying to be ironic. There are flyers up on various light poles and bus stop terminals advertising various after-parties at the kind of venues that have metal detectors at the door, and at which you might very well be stabbed for the first time. It's exciting. Take the trip with me through the preflight buildup.

Everywhere I go I see Tyson. He's on television in a deli, telling CNN's audience that he is going to "gut Kevin McBride like a fish." It is a rare moment of made-up PR-ism for Tyson. Behind those threatening words, "I'm going to gut Kevin McBride like a fish," what Tyson's really saying is, "I haven't been in a good fight in a decade, but please buy the pay-per-view because now I really need money." And he does need the money. His former manager, Steve Lott, once told me something to the effect of, "How do you go broke on ninety million dollars? Spend ninety-one million."

And so it is with Tyson, whose story you probably already know. Tyson grew up in the Brownsville section of Brooklyn, New York, robbing and thieving on the streets not just to be able to eat but also for the sheer thrill of the whole thing.[2] He then spent the early/middle parts of his young life under the tutelage of an old boxing ascetic named Cus D'Amato. This is where he learned to fight. The bob, the weave. The head movement. The vicious uppercut that you yourself have probably avoided on *Mike Tyson's PunchOut*.[3] This Tyson was impeccably trained and kept busy, so as to be kept out of trouble (only somewhat successful). It was during this time period that few of his fights ever lasted more than three minutes, and he actually knocked out Joe Frazier's son Marvis in thirty seconds and change. He appeared on the cover of *Sports Illustrated* under the headline "Kid Dynamite." Sportswriters made much of the "ghetto kid makes good" story line, which is as tired as sportswriting itself. Then came titles, marriage to actress Robin Givens, divorce, and a rape conviction. Jail time. Peter McNeeley. Ear biting.[4] Lots of fights that didn't mean anything,[5] culminating in tonight.

So Mike Tyson saying today that he is going to gut Kevin McBride like a fish is almost Mike Tyson parodying the Mike Tyson of a few years before who said of Lennox Lewis that he wanted to "eat his children." And while I have no doubt that Tyson genuinely hated Lewis and reporters, I feel none of the same conviction for McBride, who is by all accounts a big, pasty, white guy who is also pretty nice.

Mike Tyson may very well be my favorite athlete precisely because he is *usually* immune to this kind of hucksterism. The truth is, Mike Tyson, a Muslim, talks about Jesus a lot more than Christian athletes who say they talk about Jesus.

We love athletes because they make hard things look easy. We love Michael Jordan for hanging in midair, tongue waggling, and used to love Barry Bonds for hitting 98-mile-per-hour fastballs. We used to love Roger Clemens for throwing those fastballs. For athletes, their unique gifts and charisma are best showcased between the lines, where they are completely at ease and completely in control. Even watching great athletes warm up before games is a study in popular psychology. They are loose of limb. They gallop. They joke. They chew bubble gum.

I contrast this to my own (very) brief tenure as a less-than-decent athlete, which was marked by extreme fits of nervousness not only before games but also practice.[5] Game days were marked by an almost suffocating sense of tension that began building on the morning of the event and reached a nauseating crescendo at some point during the national anthem. Even if there were only fifty-nine people in the bleachers, I was convinced that those people were about to watch me send a snap over the head of the punter or the holder, and this embarrassed me to no end.

Most athletes, though, are surprisingly inarticulate about what it is that they do between those lines. We buy jock biographies and autobiographies expecting the athletes to be as charismatic in print as they are on the court, but they are rarely so.

That's because they aren't compelling communicators—just great ath-letes. Consider just two NBA all-stars a few years ago. I was shocked to find that Allen Iverson, whose game I had admired for so long—the slashes to the hoop, the hustle, and even the tats and cornrows—was quiet, sullen, and churlish in interviews. He barely removed the headphones from his ears and never made eye contact. He seemed as though he would rather have been beaten than be forced to talk about basketball.

Michael Jordan was a measure better, but not much so. He was a modern-day Mozart when it came to playing the media, and I'm pretty sure most of it happened on a subconscious level, which made it hard to be mad at Jordan for being insincere. Even today, Jordan says things cor-rectly. He says things with a smile that has sold, among other things, Gatorade, Nikes, and men's underwear. He doesn't reveal too much, but he reveals just enough to make you feel like he's revealed something.

I interviewed him during his last season as a pro basketball player, when he was a member of the Washington Wizards. His team was out of serious contention, and he was in Auburn Hills to play the Pistons. I found him in the visitor's locker room, which is almost as nice as a locker room you would find in any midsized high school or YMCA in America. Folding chairs. Metal lockers.

Jordan was here in a suit that is worth more than the car I drove to the arena. He looked regal, even splayed out on a folding chair, with a small television monitor propped in front of him.

So here's Jordan, watching game film. He gives me a quote about how "I'll miss the guys" when he's done playing ball. He then goes out and proceeds to be unbelievably competitive, even though he is almost forty and the game doesn't mean anything. His true charisma shines on the court.

My first experience covering pro baseball was a similar letdown. I was led into a huge (think small high school gymnasium) locker room in Comerica Park, home of the Detroit Tigers, with (rough count) probably fifteen empty tables and seventy-five comfortable, empty chairs in the center of the room. I was there to interview Dimitri Young, who wasn't yet in the room.

In fact, nobody was in the room, so I sat in one of those chairs. When Young arrived, I had a mostly unremarkable interview that was remarkable only in that we were both seated. I learned through an official Detroit Tigers PR wonk that reporters weren't allowed to sit anywhere in the premises—the premises being the locker room full of empty seats. We were required to stand while the athlete sits in his chair, stares at the floor, and mumbles.

All of this, of course, speaks to why we need Mike Tyson and Ricky Williams even though they have both been outwardly hostile toward the media. Their seeming hostility toward the media and their willingness to talk openly about that hostility and other things[6] is precisely what makes them interesting.

RANDOM MIKE TYSON QUOTES YOU MIGHT FIND INTERESTING:

Mike Tyson on feelings in which he says the words "emotionally and personally," which betrays the fact that he has probably been in and out of counseling his whole life: "I never saw my mother happy with me and proud of me for doing something: She only knew me as being a wild kid running the streets, coming home with new clothes that she knew I didn't pay for. I never got a chance to talk to her or know about her. Professionally, it has no effect, but it's crushing emotionally and personally."

Mike Tyson on Jesus and how Jesus would approach Mike Tyson if Jesus were around today: "I'm a Muslim, but do you think Jesus would love me? I think Jesus would have a drink with me and discuss 'Why are you acting like that?' Now, He would be cool. He would talk to me. No Christian ever did that and said [it was] in the name of Jesus even.

They'd throw me in jail and write bad articles about me and then go to church on Sunday and say Jesus is a wonderful man and He's coming back to save us. But they don't understand that when He comes back, that these crazy greedy capitalistic men are gonna kill Him again."

Mike Tyson on potentially becoming a missionary: "I want to be a missionary . . . go to Sudan, help with the relief efforts. I've lived my whole life for myself up to now."

Mike Tyson on deep books and Tolstoy: "When I was in prison, I was wrapped up in all those deep books. That Tolstoy [garbage]—people shouldn't read that stuff."

Mike Tyson on loneliness: "When I'd get up in the morning, he'd (Cus D'Amato) make me breakfast. Now he's not around anymore. I'm going to do well, but when I come down to it, who really cares? I like doing my job, but I'm not happy being victorious. I fight my heart out and give it my best, but when it's over, there's no Cus to tell me how I did, no mother to show my clippings to."

A RICKY WILLIAMS INTERLUDE

I have never met or been around Ricky Williams personally, and in all honesty, my three observations about the onetime Heisman Trophy winner, onetime star of the Miami Dolphins, and onetime Pro Bowl MVP are as follows.

First, the New Orleans Saints trading away all of their draft choices to acquire Ricky Williams with pick five of the first round in the 1999 NFL draft after his record shattering career at the University of Texas. Shortly thereafter, Williams appeared shirtless, in dreadlocks, wearing a wedding dress with coach Mike Ditka (himself in a tuxedo-as-husband-figure) on the cover of *ESPN the Magazine*. Williams made more news by hiring "Master P," a rapper also known as Percy Miller, to negotiate his rookie contract—a contract that, for all intents and purposes, turned out to be kind of a joke compared to comparable rookie deals. However, I always had a great deal of admiration for Ricky Williams and his style as an athlete. He never shied away from contact and always hit the hole hard. He also caught the ball well out of the backfield and seemed to pretty much be a selfless teammate.

Second, Ricky Williams retired (temporarily) from pro football in August 2004. As anyone who follows pro football knows, early August is when NFL teams are in training camp, right around the first weekend for preseason games. He essentially left his team high and dry, and forced them to limp through the season without the services of a starting NFL running back (no offense to Travis Minor, but Williams had run more than 3,200 yards during his previous two years). Williams retired largely because he got busted for smoking marijuana, which is no small offense. However, after having played both collegiate and minor league football, I'm more than convinced that there are a lot of pro (and college) athletes currently smoking marijuana. What made the situation tougher for Williams is that he didn't spend the time lifting weights and talking about how much he was going to quit smoking and rededicate his life to football; rather, he moved to the middle of nowhere in California (after a previous stint in middle-of-nowhere-Australia) and committed himself to becoming a yoga instructor. This drew the ire of hard-core football types. Williams became the butt of every morning-radio-talk-show host's pot joke, even though many of those selfsame hosts had probably also smoked pot but had never averaged four yards per carry in the NFL or won a Heisman trophy.

This was also the time period in which Williams was featured in a lot of TV segments accompanied by soft-focus images of him doing yoga while sitar music played in the background. It was weird. It was weird to hear words like "find myself" come out of the mouth of a 220-pound halfback instead of the usual dweeby PBS types.

My third observation with Ricky Williams happened watching him during a Mike Wallace interview on the news show *60 Minutes*. I literally stumbled upon the program—which I never watch—and was completely sucked in within a matter of minutes. Part of the reason was that Williams had a full beard, which made him look not at all like a football player, but rather like the kind of guy that holds a PhD and teaches in the urban studies department at your university. His cool-guy dreadlocks had been replaced by an afro that looked like it hadn't been styled in a long time. The other interesting part of this is that in Wallace, the show's producers had found the whitest, oldest, most establishment-ish guy to sit across the microphone from Williams, and oddly, Williams handled it like a champ.[7]

He was soft-spoken, as always, but incredibly composed and erudite for a guy who supposedly hates the media and has been diagnosed with social anxiety disorder and depression. He stressed that he would never play football again (this was during his self-imposed exile, and he would later serve a league-mandated suspension), but Wallace bet him, on the show, that he would. They bantered a little bit about whether the payout would be "lunch or dinner," to which Williams responded, "It will have to be dinner, because I'm working now." Williams later played football with the Toronto Argonauts and then the Miami Dolphins (again).

WHY I WANT TO LISTEN
TO WILLIAMS AND TYSON

It struck me that night (though not for the first time) that I would much rather listen to Ricky Williams talk about marijuana and yoga and his weaknesses than listen to Kurt Warner thank God for his Super Bowl performance.[8] I'd rather hear Mike Tyson talk through his less-than-perfect thoughts on Jesus than read another fawning feature on what a swell family guy Seahawks running back Shaun Alexander is, and by all accounts, he is—a swell guy and a good Christian.

I think this because I can see a lot of my own conflictedness in Tyson and Williams. While I've never done the things that they have, exactly, I've thought about them and felt them in my heart, making me no less needy of God's forgiveness than they are. I can relate to guys who feel angry, nervous, and self-conscious, while I have a harder time relating to Super Bowl champions for whom things appear to be going incredibly well.

RANDOM RICKY WILLIAMS QUOTES
YOU MIGHT FIND INTERESTING:

Ricky Williams on ego[9]: "I loved playing football, but the reasons I loved football were just to feed my ego. And anytime you feed your ego, it's a one-way street.[10] There were so many things I had to deal with that erased the positives I got from playing the game that it wasn't worth it. It's like eating a Big Mac and drinking a Diet Coke."

Ricky Williams on politics and professional football: "Practicing politics is like professional football. You have to be smart enough to understand the rules and stupid enough to think what you are doing is important."

Ricky Williams on being paid $3.6 million as a twenty-year-old to play professional football: "That was before taxes," Williams said. "After, it was like 2 . . . 2.4. . . . It bound me more than it freed me because now I had more things to worry about. I had more people asking for money. I thought I had to buy a house and nice cars and different things that people with money are supposed to do."

Ricky Williams on what he was reading when he was living in a $7 a day tent community in Australia, shortly after quitting pro football the first time: "Everything from nutrition to Buddhism to Jesus, to try to figure out, you know, what am I? What am I? So I just kept reading and reading. And couldn't figure out what I was, but I learned a lot."

Ricky Williams on when it's okay for someone (him) to quit playing football: "When would it have been okay for me to stop playing football?" Williams says. "When my knees went out? When my shoulders went out? When I had too many concussions? When is it okay? . . . I'm just curious. I'm just curious, because I don't understand. When is it okay to not play football anymore?"

Williams's words reveal a guy searching for answers that transcend sports: Who am I? What am I? Are my body and health important in a world where football defines me? Those are big questions of purpose and identity we all can ask—even if we don't have super athletic bodies that can earn us million dollar contracts.

Mike Tyson and Ricky Williams both seem to hold their money-making professions loosely. By thanking God profusely for touchdowns and for the opportunity to play pro football, some Christian athletes unwittingly make the game bigger than God Himself. Williams doesn't do this; and Tyson recognizes his talent will pass and other things count. For Williams and Tyson, learning not to loathe themselves, and learning something about God and the meaning of life in the process, seems to be a much bigger deal.

Hours before the Tyson fight in D.C., a fidgety kid from Los Angeles comes to my hotel room and says he plans to make a documentary about Mike Tyson. The kid has produced some Daft Punk music videos and is interested in my book. I'm interested in his movies. We're both interested in Mike Tyson because we're both Christians and we both find him utterly fascinating.

This fascination is basically driven by the fact that we both want to tell him about Jesus. We discover this shared interest somewhere between the hotel and the MCI Center where, after several hours, Mike Tyson will be knocked out by Kevin McBride, effectively ending his career.

I have been witnessing to Mike Tyson in my head all night, through the prelim fights, through Muhammad Ali's appearance, and into the press conference that Tyson bravely gives after the fight, much of which is described in greater detail in *Facing Tyson*. Tyson talks for a couple of hours, mostly about how much he hates the fight game, how much he probably deserves to go to jail, and how he would like to one day become a missionary. The word "surreal" doesn't begin to describe it.

If I could get the opportunity to witness to Tyson (and Ricky), I would tell him that he probably has a greater grasp on his own depravity and need for redemption than many of the Christians I know. I would tell him that though his sins are many and well documented (mine, too, are many—though less documented), Christ died to pay the penalty for those sins (his and mine alike), freeing us and compelling us to live Christlike lives ourselves that will end in glory when we spend eternity in heaven. I would invite him to read the book of Romans. I would ask him to call me or e-mail me to chat about it, and I would pull a sheet of paper out of my steno notebook and write: tcd@tcdkluck.com.

Then I would thank him for his honesty, and let him know that there's at least one person in sports who doesn't hate him.

NOTES

1. In this case Mike Tyson vs. Kevin McBride, which can't exactly be considered a big fight, save for the fact that it involved Tyson, who was boxing's biggest box office draw for about a decade and a half.

2. Tyson talks about punching old ladies in the face as a kid and then taking their groceries, which is really vile and unpleasant. But whereas most reformed, formerly wild pro athletes say, "I stole to put food on the table," Tyson readily admits that he did it for the rush. This reminds me a lot of Augustine's story about the pears in *The Confessions of Saint Augustine*. Augustine said, in essence, he didn't steal the pears because he needed pears; he did it because it was a thrill.

THE REASON FOR SPORTS

3. He was the first athlete with a major-release video game named after him, according to Lott.

4. Tyson rather famously took a chunk out of Evander Holyfield's ear during their second fight, which he was losing in much the same fashion with which he lost their first fight. Having discussed this with Holyfield at length in *Facing Tyson*, I won't use much space on it here, except to say that Evander Holyfield had no fear of Mike Tyson and that, I think, was the difference.

5. Botha, Norris, Francis, Golota, Nielsen, Savarese, Etienne, and Williams (Danny).

6. Like Jesus.

7. Future president of the United States and current male model/quarterback of the New England Patriots, Tom Brady, would sit across from that same microphone in a couple of years and say, of the Super Bowl, "Is this all there is?" Interesting.

8. No disrespect here to Warner, who I like, and whose game I like too.

9. The quotes by Williams, like those by Tyson, were made in a variety of settings to a variety of interviewers. They are gathered here to show these athletes have shown moments of brilliant clarity, at times followed by their doing amazingly stupid things.

10. See also the book of Ecclesiastes.

DISHONESTY
and SPORTS

NICK SABAN, JASON KIDD, AND
LETTING YOUR YES BE YES

It's not "show friends," it's "show business."

BOB SUGAR
Jerry McGuire

![peanuts]

Just two years after calling the Miami Dolphins coaching job his "dream job," head coach Nick Saban left Miami. Said Dolphins defensive end Jason Taylor of Saban's sudden exit: "Yeah, his decision was selfishly based, but at the end of the day, isn't everybody going to take the best job that's available? Find me one NFL head coach who didn't lie last year. I don't want to get too political, but we're in a war based on false pretenses. We have problems in this nation with health care and affordable housing, and how many politicians have lied about that? And people want to freak out because Nick Saban wouldn't coach a football team?"

Taylor is, in some sense, right, because who cares who coaches the Miami Dolphins? I mean, it makes great copy for sports columns and lots of entertaining debates among Dolphin fans and NFL pundit types, but, really, who cares? The Dolphins will or will not score more points than their opponents. They will still field a team whether Saban is at the helm or not, and, in fact, if veterans like Keith Traylor and Vonnie Holliday were to be believed, many of the players wanted him gone anyway because his rah-rah/yeller/screamer/college-guy routine didn't exactly play well on a veteran squad.[1] They will still sell tickets and merchandise, with or without Nick Saban.

But the distressing element of Taylor's quote can be found here: "Find me one NFL coach who didn't lie in the last year."

That statement is a problem, because the NFL coaching fraternity he speaks of includes outspoken Christians (Tony Dungy, Lovie Smith), authors or the subjects of motivational/"secret of my success"-type books (Jon Gruden, Charlie Weis, Bill Belichick), legends (Joe Gibbs, also an outspoken Christian), and many other community-leader types. Like it or not, these men are celebrities, role models, and image shapers in our culture, largely because of the amounts of money they make each year. They're not unlike CEOs in that regard. So I don't worry about whether all of these men are liars (they're not), but I am disturbed that Taylor (and probably many fans) think they're liars and *expect* them to lie.

Nick Saban signed a contract with the University of Alabama in 2007, an eight-year deal worth $32 million, making him the highest-paid football coach in the United States, college or pro. His two-year NFL record was 15–17 at the time (though his previous college record at LSU was 48–16 and one national championship). Upon leaving the Dolphins, he was called "a liar" by ESPN's Pat Forde, and "a fraud" by NFL coaching legend Don Shula.

Those harsh comments by Forde and Shula no doubt were based on statements made by Coach Saban during his final weeks as an NFL coach that seemed less than aboveboard:

- *November 27, 2006:* "When I was in college it was always about coming to the pros. This is the challenge I wanted. I had a good college job [coaching at LSU]. Why would I have left that if I was going to be interested in other college jobs?

   "I took this as a challenge. We certainly haven't seen this through and gotten where we want to go and finished the job here, so why would I be interested in something else?"

- *December 7, 2006:* "I'm flattered that they (Alabama) may have been interested in me, but it never really progressed, because we just never let it progress."

- *December 21, 2006:* "I guess I have to say it. I'm not going to be the Alabama coach. . . . I don't control what people say. I don't control what people put on [Internet blogs] or anything else. So I'm just telling you there's no significance, in my opinion, about this, about me, about any interest that I have in anything other than being the coach here."

- *December 27, 2006:* "I'm just making a rule to never comment on something like that again because every time you comment on it, it just makes for another story. So I'm not going to comment on it five years from now, and I'm not going to comment on it next week."

- *January 4, 2007*, *during the press conference introducing him as head coach of the University of Alabama:* "What I realized in the last two years is that we love college coaching because of the ability that it gives you to affect people, young people. . . . If I knew that my heart was someplace else in what I wanted to do, I don't think it would be fair to the [Dolphins] organization if I stayed."

It's worth mentioning that I certainly don't think Nick Saban is the first coach of his stature to lie to his team, the media, and the nation in this regard, and he won't be the last. I'm reminded of Central Michigan

University coach Brian Kelley who allegedly entertained a recruit in his home on the same day that he would agree to become the coach at another school, Cincinnati. He told reporters he chose Cincinnati because the new city offered "more cultural opportunities" for his family, as though Southwest Ohio was a cultural mecca of Manhattanesque proportions, just waiting to be explored.

LANDING THE STUD RECRUIT

And now Nick Saban has the title, University of Alabama head coach. Imagine, for a minute, then, that you are the parent of a potential 2008 Alabama Crimson Tide football recruit. Or better yet, imagine that you are the recruit himself. Nick Saban pulls into your neighborhood in a nice car, and comes to your doorstep in full Alabama regalia. The whole of the neighborhood is collected on their porches to see the arrival of one of the highest-paid men in America. He wears garish, heavy Bowl rings on his fingers. (He won two Sugar Bowls and one Peach Bowl title at LSU.) He comes with glossy media guides and highlight videos under arm. He lays out Alabama's sterling record of putting players into the NFL, along with his own sterling record of doing the same thing. Saban smoothes your mom, and throws a thick paw around your dad's shoulders connecting on some bit of minutia, like the fact that they are both the sons of coal miners, or state troopers, or war veterans, or schoolteachers.

Imagine now that you are Stud Recruit's father. How do you respond when your son's potential coach—the highest-paid coach in America—waxes eloquent, as coaches are wont to do, about integrity, trust, and the work ethic? Are you wooed by the bling and by the prospect of your son playing for a man who has won national titles and coached in the NFL?

As the Stud Recruit, however, you have some leverage. The precedent for dishonesty that has been set by Saban and other college coaches is nothing new under the sun—it is plain old sin nature. On the other hand, athletes have done their part to play down to that level. Take, for example, the case of Jerrell Powe, a five-star stud defensive tackle targeted in 2005 by, among others, Auburn, LSU, and Ole Miss. Powe, who would probably have no business being admitted to any of these fine institutions on his academic merit (he didn't actually graduate from high school on time),[2] had in his favor the fact that he was a 6-foot-3, 321-pound man-child who could cover 40 yards in a remarkably quick 5.1 seconds.

Like many high school all-Americans, Powe was invited to play in the nationally televised Army all-American game. As a part of the festivities, many athletes perform surreal sideline sideshows, such as pulling a T-shirt or cap out of a duffel bag to reveal their four-year academic institution of choice. As I wrote in my book *Game Time*, these vignettes have taken on a reality-TV-meets-game-show flavor, and are at the same time tributes to the already massively developed egos of the athletes and also very sad. Imagine such treatment for the valedictorian of your high school, or the chemistry major-to-be down the street—staging his or her own press conference to announce where she'll continue her chemistry studies for the next four years . . . five if she studies abroad. I know . . . sounds surreal. But just imagine: "Ladies and gentlemen, I'm Lillian Wong and I'll be studying molecular biology at Stanford" (pulls on ball cap). Applause.

Prior to the all-American game, Powe had told Internet pundits that he would be an Auburn Tiger—which doesn't mean much because, as I've since learned, players lie to these sites all the time about subjects like their GPA, 40-yard-dash time, size, and high school statistics. At any rate, Powe volunteered to make his commitment[3] on television, at which point he pulled a purple LSU Tigers cap out of a bag and said, "It's LSU, baby!"

Needless to say, this sent those inhabiting the recruiting world— many of whom, admittedly, have no life—into a tailspin. Not the least of these spinning were coaches at Auburn and Ole Miss, both of whom thought they had the big defensive tackle sewn up. Powe's comments to the media were illuminating: "I don't know why I committed to LSU," he said. "That isn't my final choice. It might change on Signing Day. It's just a commitment. My decision's subject to change. I might sign with LSU, Auburn, or Ole Miss. I've just got to do what's best for me."

Like Nick Saban, Powe just thought he was doing "what's best for him." He was either a confused kid, overwhelmed by the pressure of recruiting, or he was a jaded cynic, playing a big joke on the big-money machine he was about to become a cog in. Either way, we'll never know.

Again, you have heard that it was said to the people long ago, "Do not break your oath, but keep the oaths you have made to the Lord." But I tell you, Do not swear at all: either by heaven, for it is God's throne; or by the earth, for it is his footstool; or by Jerusalem, for it is the city of the Great King. And do not swear by your head, for you cannot make even one hair white or black. Simply let your "Yes" be "Yes," and your "No," "No"; anything beyond this comes from the evil one.

Jesus, in Matthew 5:33–37

It disturbs me that what might be the best sports movie ever made, *Jerry McGuire*, is based on characters—sports agents—who have become stars in their own right over the course of the last several years. Agents have already been roundly vilified in print, so I'll abstain from piling on. I have a literary agent myself, and find him very helpful when it comes to doing some things that range from bad to downright-incapable-of, like math and asking for things (money).

He bears little resemblance to the characters in *Jerry McGuire*, though I like those characters too.

I mention agents only because they have brought to light another disturbing trend in sports—the midcontract renegotiation.

During the 2007–2008 NBA season, New Jersey Nets point guard Jason Kidd allegedly faked a headache so that he wouldn't have to play in a scheduled game, and later referred to the incident as a "work stoppage." Life is hard in today's NBA. How can we forget Stephen Jackson's impassioned plea after David Stern's dress code ruling, in which he explained, "It's just tough, man, knowing that all of a sudden you have to have a dress code out of nowhere. They don't want your chains to be out, all gaudy and shiny. But that's the point of them." Well, somebody finally explained the point of chains. Jackson would add, "I feel like if they want us to dress a certain way, they should pay for our clothes."

Finally, somebody said what so many were thinking. This is the NBA world we live in. Why should NBA players, who make on average $3.7 million, have to pay for their own business casual?

HOW TO HANDLE A LABOR DISPUTE

So it's easy to understand Jason Kidd's unique dilemma when it comes to labor disputes. Let's get a handle on the Kidd situation, and then compare it with labor disputes in other places:

Date: December 5, 2007

Group: Jason Kidd

Annual Salary (reported, HoopsHype.com): $19.728 million

Cause: Sat out an NBA regular season game against the New York Knicks, a game that his team lost, reportedly seeking a trade or a contract extension.

Quote: "I have a migraine."

Date: July 3, 1835

Group: Paterson, New Jersey, children employed in silk mills

Cause: Seeking an eleven-hour day, and a six-day workweek.

Comment: Similarities to Kidd's situation abound, in that both events happened in New Jersey, and both involve people who sometimes act like children. In the case of the silk workers, it was real children.

Date: 1834 and 1836

Group: Female mill workers, Lowell, Massachusetts

Cause: Striking against a reduction in wages, which ranged from $3 to $5 per week.

Comment: The strike failed and within a few days the women were back at work, with reduced wages. Apparently, many women tried the "I have a migraine" method, but callous mill owners made them come to work anyway.

Date: July 1, 1922

Group: Nationwide railroad shop workers. In the Great Railroad Strike of 1922, the shop workers went on strike, leaving vacant some 400,000 positions. Apparently the strike died out, as many shop workers made individual deals with local railroads.

Cause: Reversal of a proposed seven-cent wage decrease.

Comment: Those railroad workers should try the day-in-and-day-out grind of life in the NBA, which includes taking chartered planes to five-star accommodations, receiving hundreds of dollars in cash per diem, and trying to look good in David Stern's "business casual." Then we'll see who's complaining.

Date: October 6, 1986

Group: Flight attendants

Cause: Female flight attendants who had been fired from United Airlines for getting married win an eighteen-year lawsuit and receive some $37 million in back-pay settlement.

Comment: Thirty-seven million dollars! Now we're talking. That's J-Kidd money. However, those dollars were divided between 1,725 flight attendants.

Unlike many of these examples, Kidd got the trade he so desperately lobbied for, and is now doing his thing as a member of the Dallas Mavericks. The lesson here, kids: If you're unsatisfied with your own multimillion dollar contract, you can always demand to renegotiate during the season or force a trade by staging your own "work stoppage."

So how do meekness and humility jive with the Drew Rosenhaus[4] ethic of getting yours? As a fan, should you expect the Christian athlete to ask for more, since others do? How does the Christian athlete survive in the market-driven economy that is professional sports?

CONTRACT NEGOTIATIONS
AND THE CHRISTIAN ATHLETE

A Christian athlete could follow the example of outspoken Christian, *Sports Spectrum* magazine cover boy, and current Boston Red Sox right fielder J. D. Drew, who along with agent Scott Boras publicly guaranteed that they would not sign a rookie contract for less than $10 million when the Philadelphia Phillies chose Drew the second overall pick in the 1997 MLB draft. True to his word (at least his yes was yes), Drew held out for the year and was drafted the following season by St. Louis.[5] When the team traveled to Veteran's Stadium to face the Phillies, J. D. was booed heartily and even pelted with "D" batteries.

The one constant in Drew's career is that he has been among the least-popular (from a fan perspective) players on his ball club, wherever he has played, which seems to me to be a shame for a Christian player. The Bible says that "we'll be hated for what we believe," but I doubt that covers our convictions regarding our first big league contract and its megasize.

So was Drew in the wrong when he sat out to demand multiple millions from his first big-league club? Honestly, I'm not sure. This is probably a gray area, of which there are many in adult life. If anything, he's guilty of appearing to be almost unprecedentedly greedy, which may have ruined his witness among the majority of MLB fans, most of whom (myself included) are still middle-to-working class and have to scrimp just to be able to afford a couple of tickets to the ballpark. Forgive me for not being excited to hear about the testimony and witness of a guy who once held out for ten million dollars. I don't know that we'd have much in common.

Or should we follow in the footsteps of one Chad Johnson, wide receiver for the Cincinnati Bengals? On February 4, 2008, following a Pro Bowl season, Johnson announced through his agent (Rosenhaus) that he would indeed play in 2008 (there was some talk of a Johnson work stoppage), but that it may not be with the Bengals. There has been some discussion as to whether Johnson's angst is over his contract (maybe) or the Bengals and their ineptitude (probably).

So, hypothetically, where does the Christian marquee receiver (if there is one) fit into this equation? A receiver who was probably lied to by his college coach, and may be dealing with the expectations of a less-than-ethical agent? Or more realistically, where do you, the Christian fan, fit in? Can you shelve your cynicism for long enough to go to your local NFL stadium and watch Chad Johnson pluck footballs out of the air and run past defenses, which is, in his defense, a pretty doggone beautiful and impressive thing to watch? Can you put on your Crimson hat and cheer for the fiery Nick Saban, questionable ethics and all, on Saturday afternoon?

My answer is probably yes, for the same reason that we can enjoy

Ocean's Eleven even though Brad Pitt has been a philandering husband, and *The Rolling Stones* though Nick, Keith, and Charlie have all had well-documented losing battles with cocaine, heroin, et al. The movies are entertaining and the music is still, well, sweet. Pitt is still an amazing actor regardless of his failures as a chaste husband. I still like him, just like I still like Ocho Cinco[6] even though he's basically a greedy clown. But he's a greedy clown with a penchant for catching beautiful touchdowns and doing it in a not-unentertaining way.

But to whom much has been given, much is required, and I guess I require more from my brothers and sisters in Christ, in sports. My hope is that, unlike the Dolphins' Jason Taylor, we stop short of unbridled cynicism, and expect a little bit more out of our Christian athletes (and coaches). And we hope that there are at least a few for whom commitment isn't just another signing-day platitude, made to be broken. And for whom contract is not only a covenant with their team, but something that their fans and teammates can count on.

My hope for these athletes is that keeping their word will result in their being paid what they're worth in the marketplace, and being blessed spiritually in the process.

NOTES

1. It's worth noting that this isn't the first time this has happened to a college coach. When Lou Holtz left North Carolina for the New York Jets in 1976, he caused a near mutiny among the players for wanting, among other things, to make them learn a fight song. Holtz left the Jets with one game remaining in '76, and his record was 3-10.

2. As his mother explained after schools competed for Powe's favor while he was academically ineligible, "Jerrell really is a good child, but he just can't read." See Wright Thompson, "Powe to Stay True to His School," *ESPN Insider*, January 14, 2007, at http://sports.espn.go.com/ncaa/recruiting/news/story?id=2731346.

3. Commitment, defined: a freely chosen inner resolve to follow through with a course even though difficulty arises. It is a strong resolution but, because humans are limited, not absolute. Commitment, resolution, and conviction have similar strength of intent.

4. Rosenhaus is a very successful NFL agent who represents a number of A-list stars. He is widely believed to have been the inspiration for the sharky Bob Sugar character in *Jerry McGuire*, who I have to admit is one of my favorite characters in all of American film despite his less-than-desirable personal qualities.

5. Cardinals manager Tony LaRussa later questioned Drew's passion for the game, saying that it seemed Drew had "decided to settle for 75 percent" of his talent.

6. Chad Johnson's uniform has number 85, *ocho cinco* in Spanish, and Johnson's preferred nickname.

5

WHAT MIGHT
HAVE BEEN

TONY DUNGY AND
GAMES OF INCHES

On any given Sunday you're gonna win or you're gonna lose. The
point is—can you win or lose like a man?

TONY D'AMATO
Any Given Sunday

I grew up in east central Indiana and, as such, have always had a great
vantage point with which to watch the several Christian colleges
there operate. Christian colleges, like the rest of us in the evangelical
world, get excited when presented with opportunities to co-opt another
evangelical's success as a way to promote our own success.[1] I've
watched with interest, then, the co-opting of former Indianapolis Colts
head coach Tony Dungy in the wake of the Colts Super Bowl victory
after the 2006 season, and the release of Tony Dungy's bestselling book,
Quiet Strength.

This weekend I received news that Indiana Wesleyan University is
honoring Dungy with an induction into their "Society of World Changers," which according to the release "honors people making a difference in the arts, athletics, government or the business world and doing

so in a Christ-like manner." The honor will include two life-sized busts of Dungy—one to be placed on campus and one, again according to the release, "for the Colts arena."

Let me point out that I think a lot of Tony Dungy. I interviewed him in *Sports Spectrum* magazine pre-Super Bowl and found him to be truly kind and humble—a rarity in the Christian sports business. Dungy, according to his players, is a true father figure and an example of the gospel at work in real life. He seems to have a more healthy perspective on his accomplishments than many of the people who laud him for those accomplishments. And as an athlete I can speak to the fact that, behind closed doors, he'll be made fun of for the bust, and he will have a chuckle at the fact that people are bronze-busting him for essentially being good at coaching the cover-2 defense.

Still, the sainthood of Tony Dungy leaves me wondering what would have happened had Reggie Wayne dropped that pass against New England in the 2006 AFC Championship. You'll recall that Wayne caught, bobbled, and then ultimately caught this ball, which led to the Colts narrowly defeating future genius Bill Belichick and the Patriots, which led to them defeating the Chicago Bears and their own outspoken evangelical coach, Lovie Smith, in the Super Bowl.

If Wayne drops his pass or, for that matter, if New England wide receiver Reche Caldwell catches two of the potential touchdown passes that he dropped, Tony Dungy's first book sells 20,000 copies instead of one million, and Indiana Wesleyan gives their Society of World Changers Award, and the attendant busts, to someone not affiliated with the Indianapolis Colts, the team that would now have the stigma of never being able to win the big one. Tony Dungy would retire as a very successful NFL coach who never won a Super Bowl. Peyton Manning is christened as The Quarterback Who Can't Win the Big One, gets maybe a third of the endorsement opportunities he has currently, and has to see his younger, less talented brother, Eli, win the Big One for the New York Giants the following year.

Meanwhile, Tom Brady, his perfect cheekbones, and the Pats ascend to "Living Legends" status a year earlier. Bill Belichick is even more of a genius. Perhaps Reche Caldwell stays in the league. And we have one less evangelical coach to co-opt.

By now almost every baseball fan knows the cautionary tale that is Steve Bartman. Bartman, you'll recall, is the fan who intervened with a foul ball that, if caught, could have led to a Chicago Cubs victory over the Florida Marlins, in a game they were five outs from winning in October 2003. Since the incident there have been the attendant death threats, the "death to Bartman" websites, and also the outpourings of forgiveness from current Cubs, former Cubs, and other public-figure types.

The thing I remember most about Bartman was his regularness. He was a slightly geeky but mostly normal looking, bundled-up, bespectacled, radio-wearing Cubs fan. He didn't look like a boozy, affluent, Chicago northside yuppie, nor was he a college-aged-frat-boy out for a night of carousing with his buddies. Actually, he reminded me a little bit of myself, and a lot of the other Cubs fans in my life. Guys who probably would have done the same thing in the same situation.

Yet Bartman's becoming the lightning rod for a hundred years of Cubs postseason futility has become the stuff of legend. Bartman's parents changed their phone number, and Bartman is still occasionally hounded by reporters like ESPN's Wayne Drehs, who staked out the parking garage at his office complex in order to ask him about the incident. Bartman, I learned in the ESPN piece, has a legal team. All of this to say that people care. People care about the Cubs. People's moods are affected by the Cubs, and how often they do or don't win. This is what it means to be a fan. You care.

SWEET INSPIRATION

Perhaps more interesting is the fact that Bartman still has his house in the suburbs, and still works in a Chicago office somewhere where he is forced to dangle his name, Steve Bartman, from a security badge on his belt. He stayed in Chicago when people expected Bartman to leave the country in shame or at least request a transfer to a nonbaseball city where he could then hang his head in shame.

This strikes me as incredibly inspirational.

We love inspirational stories in sports. We love underdogs. Had Bartman watched the game on television that night, and had the Cubs managed to get the five outs they needed to win the game, and had they[2] managed to go on to play in, and maybe actually win, the World Series that year, we would be talking about how inspirational they were for undoing decades worth of losing. Human interest features would have been written about the faiths of the Christian players on the Cubs. As it is now, it's hard to remember much about that Cubs team, other than Bartman, who still has to confront the day-to-day monotony of being in his late twenties, driving to an office building, and swiping a security badge day after day—only he has to do it with the additional emotional/ psychic weight of being The Guy Who Ruined It for The Cubs and The City of Chicago. He has to see the cocked eyebrows in the hallways, and endure the witty comments every time he is introduced to someone at a meeting or conference. He has to live with the fact that he will never make a name for himself, probably, outside this incident. The fact that he'll never enjoy viewing the freshly cut green grass at Wrigley Field again, as he walks up the ramp to find his seat. He'll never take in a Cubs game with his dad in the bleachers.

In sports we like to talk about athletes dealing with adversity like knee injuries or imperfect weather conditions. Steve Bartman deals with real adversity that, for most of us, a mountain of Prozac couldn't put a dent in. We should be bronze-busting him somewhere.

There's a rap song out now whose lyrics state, "I'm Mike Jones, don't act like you don't know my name." Mike Jones is one of the plainest names in America. There are a million of them across the country. But one Mike Jones—the journeyman linebacker for the St. Louis Rams—made Kurt Warner and his wife famous. Jones was the guy who stopped Tennessee Titans wide receiver Kevin Dyson on the one-inch line[3] in the Super Bowl that made Kurt Warner and his stocking-shelves-at-Hi Vee-to-arena-league-to-Super Bowl-championship story the stuff of inspirational, evangelical legend.

Warner seemed to be on the cover of *Sports Spectrum* and *Sharing the Victory* every three months for a couple of years straight. He wrote a book called *All Things Possible,* which seemed to come out about a week after his Super Bowl victory. I like Warner, and I especially respect what he's been through as a player recently, persevering through injuries and bad teams to take the Arizona Cardinals to the Super Bowl in 2009. The problem with Warner's exceptional story was timing. His *All Things Possible* experience coincided with the end of my own football career—an end that came due to injuries and, quite honestly, my just not being very good. For me, nothing felt possible.

Jones played college ball at Missouri, and then played eleven largely unremarkable seasons for the Rams, Raiders, and Steelers. He finished with nine sacks, eight interceptions, and many tackles in 183 games, none of them more important than the one on Dyson in Super Bowl. Dyson finished his six NFL seasons with 124 catches and eleven touchdowns. He played for four teams and, for a first round draft choice (16th overall, 1998), is considered a disappointment.

Let's wonder for a moment what happens if Mike Jones is a tenth of a second late to Kevin Dyson on that most important snap, and Dyson is able to glide over the Astroturf unfettered into Super Bowl glory. Would Kurt Warner's story be any less inspiring? If Kevin Dyson falls in the forest and no one hears it, does it make a sound?

I think what I like most about Tony Dungy is the fact that he doesn't have any canned, inspirational phrases ready for our interview. This interview with Dungy is something of a full-circle experience for me. As mentioned in the introduction, I worked for the Indianapolis Colts in training camp back in the early 90s and haven't been back since. I see my old boss, from a distance. I see several familiar faces and revel in the familiar thwack of pad on pad.

Dungy radiates true humility when he approaches me after practice. The fact that he approaches me at all is nothing short of miraculous in a media world in which athletes are often cordoned off by an army of heel-nipping PR wonks. The thing I appreciate most about Dungy is that he seems to really get how lucky he is. He knows the by-inches nature of winning and losing in the NFL. And, like most coaches, he's done his time climbing the ladder, with stops at the University of Minnesota, Pittsburgh, Kansas City, and then the Vikings before landing his first head coaching job in Tampa.

"God has expectations for you in this business," he said that day, in a reflection on personal holiness that could have just as easily come out of a John Piper sermon. "You're a lamp, and how you carry yourself is very important in the midst of personal challenges."

What personal challenges?

STAYING HUMBLE

"Remaining humble when you do well, and keeping a decent attitude when you're losing," he answered. "You get the sense in this league that not everyone can end up the big winner. At the end of a season you have to evaluate the spiritual side of what you accomplish."

I get the sense that in life not everyone can end up the Big Winner, and I appreciate Dungy giving voice to that fact. Often evangelicals like telling the stories of those who have ended up Big Winners, when in fact, many of us end up somewhere between "anonymous" and "loser." Life is full of unfulfilled dreams, sick children, boring cubicles, lost jobs, death, and difficult situations sent our way to, I believe, grow us in sanctification.

What makes Dungy a truly admirable Christian coach of athletes is that he doesn't try to make his own greatness overshadow God's, even in "humility." As anyone knows who has watched any amount of sports, there is real humility, and then there's "athlete humility." Athlete humility uses even the act of being humble as a reminder of the individual greatness of that particular athlete. Example: "He's so humble! He's so down-to-earth! Look at the way he delivered turkeys to needy families on Thanksgiving and just happened to be photographed by three news channels and a magazine crew."

Paul says that they'll know us by our fruit. And Dungy's conduct in Super Bowl victory and in times of great loss, as evidenced by the death of his son, speak to the presence of Christ in his life. It is this real fruit that is, I think, truly world changing.

NOTES

1. See also endorsements on the back cover of books.
2. That's a lot of "had theys," which suggests that the Cubs probably wouldn't have managed to pull off all of these things.
3. This is now known as "The Tackle," which is further proof of the sports world's obsession with naming/labeling (see also The Drive, The Catch, The Shot Heard Round the World, etc.).

6

IS THIS
ALL THERE IS?

TOM BRADY AND THE
MIXED BLESSINGS OF BLESSING

I never said I was a golden god . . . or did I?

RUSSELL HAMMOND
Almost Famous

Tom Brady is hot. Let's just put that out there, because it's the elephant in the room. So a few years ago when I was barely making it as a writer, living in a very working-class, blue-collar section[1] of Lansing, a complimentary subscription to *Gentleman's Quarterly* began arriving on my doorstep, and continued to do so for about six months. If you're not familiar with it, *GQ* is the men's equivalent of *Cosmopolitan*— a magazine that, no matter how attractive or successful you may be, never fails to make you feel infinitely more terrible about yourself as a result of reading it. It features, mostly, articles about guys who are hotter, richer, and more talented than you are, as well as sidebars on women and gadgets you'll never have.

Anyway. One morning, in the pile of midwinter slush that really never goes away on doorsteps in Lansing, was a special *GQ* issue that seemed to be mostly devoted to Tom Brady and his attendant hotness. If you're not familiar (again), Tom Brady is the quarterback of the New England Patriots, and has won three Super Bowls, two Super Bowl MVPs, at least one supermodel (probably more), four Pro Bowl selections, and is widely considered the best active quarterback, and by some the best to have ever played the game. He played collegiately at Michigan, where he split time with a quarterback named Drew Henson who was supposed to be "All That" but is now out of the two leagues— NFL and Major League Baseball.

I pick the magazine out of the snow and realize that the good people at *GQ* thought enough of this issue to wrap it in plastic, to protect it from just these elements. I peel back the plastic and open it to find pictorials of Brady doing incredibly hot things like shearing sheep and riding a horse. I detect a serious outdoor theme. Lots of flannel and sheepskin type clothing. Lantern jaw. Stubble. A David Beckham–style shaved head. I think there's a lobster trap in there somewhere. A very Cape Codish outdoors vibe. An "early spring in the Hamptons" kind of vibe. Good grief. Brady is hot.[2]

I carry the issue in and lay it out somewhere in the living room to see if my wife will comment. She doesn't. I ask her if she thinks Tom Brady is hot,[3] to which she replies "The Midwestern jock-beefcake thing really doesn't do it for me." I think she's probably lying. To which I reply, "You just basically described the look I've been trying to pull off for most of my life."

In fact, being Tom Brady is what most men everywhere are trying to pull off. He's an exceptional athlete—envied by men and fancied by women everywhere. He's at the top of his food chain, professionally. He has a worldwide audience at his disposal whenever he wants to comment on anything which, refreshingly, is almost never, and when he does (comment) it's almost never interesting. Brady is at his most poignant when he's picking apart a cover-2 defense or using his chiseled features to sell a credit card or a razor blade. Tom Brady is meant for being looked at.

THE ULTIMATE PRIZE. AND THEN . . .

One of the few interesting statements uttered by Brady came after Super Bowl number three, when he was interviewed on *60 Minutes*. The interviewer asked Brady what he felt after winning pro football's ultimate prize, no doubt expecting him to say something along the elation-at-being-the-best or culmination-of-hard-work lines. Standard athlete stuff.

Instead, Brady said something along the lines of "Is this all there is?" It was classic book-of-Ecclesiastes stuff, and for the first time I became interested in Brady other than simply being jealous of him and therefore wishing that he would get crushed by a 260-pound blitzing linebacker.

Brady became interesting because he gave voice to something that usually only comes out in private—the fact that accomplishments/riches/fame/glory often leave their recipient lacking. I'm not happy that Brady is less than happy, I'm just proud of him for voicing it so honestly.

In Ecclesiastes 6: 1–2, the Teacher/narrator expresses a similar sentiment when he writes: "I have seen another evil under the sun, and it weighs heavily on men: God gives a man wealth, possessions and honor, so that he lacks nothing his heart desires, but God does not enable him to enjoy them, and a stranger enjoys them instead. This is meaningless, a grievous evil." He goes on to write in verse 7: "All man's efforts are for his mouth, yet his appetite is never satisfied."

Ecclesiastes is the first book of the Bible I can ever remember truly being moved by, simply because it makes absolute sense to me. I can absolutely relate to what the Teacher was experiencing and writing about, even though I haven't experienced a fraction of the success, fame, fortune, sex, and pleasure he writes about. But I've experienced enough to know that it doesn't satisfy or fill the void in the way that God can.

In a way, we're the strangers enjoying Brady's successes. And in a way dreaming about being Tom Brady is better than actually being Tom Brady, with its attendant problems, challenges, emptiness, etc. Hence the well-worn cliché that says the only thing worse than not living your dreams is living your dreams. Sports fans, especially Christian sports fans, seem to take undue pleasure in wondering aloud why athletes get into trouble. We say things like, "Why, if you were making a million dollars a year, would you _____ [4]?" I think the answer lies in Brady's statement. Athletes, just like the rest of us, don't stop to think "I shouldn't _____ because I'm already Tom Brady and being Tom Brady is pretty amazing." That's not how the minds of athletes work. They want more because they want more.

THE BOOK WITHOUT A HAPPY ENDING

I remember wondering why Joe Namath got drunk and tried to kiss Suzy Kolber on Monday Night Football a few years ago. I love Joe Namath the player, and I love Joe Namath the cultural icon, yet this had to be one of the most startlingly awkward moments in televised sports history. I was disappointed. I wondered why he couldn't have just been content to be Joe Namath—icon, legendary quarterback. The answer is the same reason I'm not content to be Ted Kluck sometimes.

It's because he couldn't find his identity in himself, just as I'm not always finding my joy and my identity in Christ.

I think I also love Ecclesiastes because it isn't a "happy ending" book. If Ecclesiastes were written today and published for a Christian audience, "the Teacher" would have become a Christian, his darkness and depression would have immediately lifted, and he would have still gotten to keep his money and esteem. The teacher of Ecclesiastes would have become an in-demand, if not somewhat morose and maudlin, conference speaker, and would have been forced to produce study guides to go along with the new "happy endings" Ecclesiastes. Sometimes it happens that way, but often it doesn't, and I think the book of Ecclesiastes is written for the rest of us.

The teacher of Ecclesiastes is worried that all his toil will be for naught. He's worried it will just be forgotten, and that the fruits of his labor will be turned over to someone less competent and more lazy. But the Teacher expresses a desire to love his work. My hope for Brady is that despite his post–Super Bowl blahs, he's able to enjoy the little, sublime things about quarterbacking—what it feels like to throw a perfect ball, the oddity that is twenty feet pointed at you in the huddle, or a perfect audible in a perfect situation.

The end of the book of Ecclesiastes is especially telling. Rather than encouraging the author to dwell on his pain, or to find himself, verses 13–14 of chapter 12 says, "Now all has been heard; here is the conclusion of the matter: Fear God and keep his commandments, for this is the whole duty of man. For God will bring every deed into judgment, including every hidden thing, whether it is good or evil."

NOTES

1. My neighbor never wore a shirt, and was not the kind of person you'd generally be okay with seeing not wearing a shirt. He also had a not-quite-functional snowmobile in his garage that he liked to rev up in the middle of the night sometimes. I'd like to say I really did a great job of "doing life" alongside this guy and witnessing to him, but . . . not really.

2. So hot he's featured as "the face" on Stetson cologne and aftershave and does commercials.

3. I'm not gay.

4. Get into a fight at a strip club . . . drink and drive . . . show up to camp out of shape . . . beat up your girlfriend . . . get thrown out of a game, etc.

7

PRIDE *and the*
MIXED BLESSING
of CURSES

THE INCREDIBLE BULK (BUST):
TONY MANDARICH

I believe that our only curses are the ones
that are self-imposed. . . . We, all of us, dig our own holes.

COACH GARY GAINES
Friday Night Lights (the movie)

he man from tomorrow is taking his drugs." That's the first line of
the landmark *Sports Illustrated* story on Tony Mandarich, from
April 24, 1989. The drugs that particular sentence referred to included
caffeine supplements that Mandarich used to psych up before work-
outs at the old Powerhouse Gym in East Lansing, Michigan, where he
was a demigod. But the subtext is undeniable. The subtext being that
the Man from Tomorrow got that way thanks in no small part to anabolic steroids.

I'm reading the *SI* piece, listening to old rock stars like Motley Crue,
Guns N' Roses, and the LA Guns,[1] and trying to channel some of the
vibe that Tony Mandarich channeled back in the late 1980s when guys
were nothing if they didn't have long, stringy hair and a GNR poster
somewhere in their room. I listened to Axl Rose when I lifted because

Sports Illustrated told me that Mandarich did the same. Such was the pull of a huge Canadian lineman over young, Midwestern males in the 1980s.

It's Thanksgiving weekend 2008, and I'm in my office, which is where I always go to escape awkward family-gathering type situations. One of the hidden blessings of self-employment is that I can always retreat into my office and that retreat can be seen as a virtuous hard-work sort of maneuver. When really it's just escapism. At any rate, this was the Thanksgiving that I became Facebook friends with former Big Ten legend and NFL "bust" [2] Tony Mandarich. If you're not familiar, Facebook is an Internet phenomenon, a social networking utility that allows you to connect with different people in different places. Now, there are two kinds of sportswriters in the world—the sloppy, gushy, just-want-to-be-in-the-presence-of-athletes kind, and the cynical kind. I'm the cynical kind, usually. But connecting with Mandarich on Facebook gave me a serious jolt of giddy-fan vibes.

Mandarich, you may recall, played offensive tackle for the Rose Bowl champion Michigan State Spartans back in the late 1980s and was the subject of a *Sports Illustrated* cover story anointing him "The Incredible Bulk." Mandarich was supposedly the picture of perfection as an offensive tackle and certainly looked the part, shirtless, on the SI cover. He was going to revolutionize the position because he had the physique and performance of a sprinter, while also carrying 330 pounds on his substantial frame. Mandarich was colorful. He loved the band Guns N' Roses, referred to Green Bay as "a village," and offered to kick Mike Tyson's (expletive). He was a bodybuilder. He had been to California.

It almost goes without saying for me to say that "The Incredible Bulk" cover was on my own teenage bedroom wall, as it was on the walls of thousands of high school kids nationwide. Mandarich became a symbol for something, and that something was strength. Independence. Rock star-ness. And he was white. Mandarich, to me, was the Great White Hope because he was perhaps the first white athlete during my formative years to combine serious athletic achievement with above-average coolness. This wasn't something that most white guys could even dream of pulling off. Up to that point the most significant white-athlete contributions came from guys who drove race cars, or were Larry Bird. None of us were trying to look like Larry Bird in high school.

BIGGER, FASTER, STRONGER, COOLER

"It was a great feeling," Mandarich says, of being bigger, faster, stronger, cooler, and more feared and famous than any other player in college football. "Years of hard work were starting to pay off for me at Michigan State. Goals I had set as a freshman in high school were starting to be realized, and I felt like I was on top of the world."

People forget that Mandarich, who recently came clean regarding his collegiate steroid use in a *Showtime* interview with Armen Keteyian and simply confirming what almost everyone already knew, was incredibly driven and goal-oriented, and had an amazing work ethic. The presence of steroids in a story like Mandarich's almost diminishes the insane amount of hard work that goes into being a Division I college athlete, much less an elite one. Mandarich was named to the AP All-American team in 1988, and was named Big Ten Lineman of the Year twice. The piece in *SI* may have been the beginning of the end for Mandarich, who in many ways was an insecure, self-destructive rock star trapped in an elite left tackle's muscular body. "I've never used them, let's leave it at that," Mandarich said of steroids in that article, but he admitted to Keteyian that he cheated to beat drug tests before the 1988 Rose Bowl.

"As a junior he could have started on any of our Super Bowl teams," said Michigan State head coach George Perles, who coached with the

Steelers in the 1970s, in the *SI* piece. "He may be the best offensive tackle ever. He's certainly the best since the game changed the blocking rules. Before that, you had to play without your arms, and it didn't matter how strong your bench press was. [Mandarich has pressed 545 pounds.] He's faster than any offensive lineman in pro football. There's probably nobody faster in the *world* at his weight. This is a different player. We'll never have another."

"I can't believe the impact it made," Mandarich says of the *Sports Illustrated* cover. "You have no idea how many people have told me that they had it on their wall. It was awesome. But after I left MSU and moved to California, I began a period of life filled with arrogance, fear, and a certain amount of cockiness."

Pride goes before destruction, and a haughty spirit before stumbling. It is better to be humble in spirit with the lowly than to divide the spoil with the proud. . . .

A man's pride will bring him low, but a humble spirit will obtain honor.

Proverbs 16:18–19; 29:23 NASB

What is meant by the word *bust*? What does it mean to be a bust? A bust, in sports vernacular, is a player who was drafted ahead of other players (and subsequently paid multimillions of dollars) but didn't end up being nearly as good as those players ahead of whom he was drafted. For example, Mandarich had the misfortune of being drafted ahead of Barry Sanders, Derrick Thomas, Deion Sanders, and Andre Rison, which means that every April when ESPN.com's purveyors of snark[3] put together their All-Time Busts lists for Page 2, he has to see his mug next to some clever copy about how much he reeked in Green Bay. Ditto for Foxsports, AOL, and SI.com. This will happen for him every April until the return of Christ. Other famous busts include Sam Bowie (basketball, drafted ahead of Michael Jordan), and Ryan Leaf, the ill-fated Chargers QB who will always be compared with Peyton Manning.

The word *bust* is also just another way to say Very Public Failure. Most of us are intimately involved with feelings of private failure; we probably experience them every day. Many of us have felt brief periods of mildly public failure as well. As an author, reading a bad review of one of my books is usually a great way to ruin at least a day, sometimes (often) more. When I read these reviews, I sometimes want to just lay in bed and feel horrible, and sometimes—I admit it—I want to find the author of the review and smash him in the face. Either way, these are terrible feelings. Failure hurts. Failure is personal. It's these semipublic author failings that have given me a new appreciation for NFL and NBA draft busts and what they go through.

Mandarich's second-most memorable *SI* cover featured another photograph—this time of him wearing a Green Bay Packers uniform, with the headline "The NFL's Incredible Bust." He spent three largely disappointing years in Green Bay marked by inconsistency, apathy, and attitude—but not the winsome, marketable kind of attitude; rather, the kind that draws resentment from teammates and coaches. This period could perhaps be best summed up by a play involving the late Reggie White, then of the Philadelphia Eagles. White performed his famous "hump" move, catching Mandarich under the left arm and tossing him aside like a rag doll. Later he was called "a façade," by future Chicago Bears Hall of Fame defensive tackle Dan Hampton, who added, "He's pathetic."

"People who say the bust label doesn't bother them are lying," he says. "It bothers me. Do I lose sleep over it? No. Does it bother me? Absolutely. The years in Green Bay were bust years. I agree with that and accept it. But it bothers me when journalists don't look at the

Indianapolis years as a part of my career. It bothers me when they fail to do their due diligence in that area, just because it will diminish the impact of the piece." (On Mandarich's Indy years, see the section, "Time to Make Amends.")

"It was crushing," he says of the Green Bay failure. "I was addicted to painkillers and drinking daily. That lifestyle comes with a lot of paranoia. Being a bust is bad enough, but my solution at the time was to take more pills to try to numb it."

Mandarich identifies California as the genesis of his shift in mindset. He moved there during the spring of his senior year to train for the NFL draft with the reigning Mr. America. "The people I surrounded myself with were different," he says. "For the most part I surrounded myself with great people at MSU—I had great coaches and teammates who were what I would call solid, Midwestern people. When I got to L.A., I started to believe all of my press, and my arrogance skyrocketed." Mandarich called himself "a slug" during the Green Bay years, and spoke of only desiring the next fix. He lived only for getting high and feeding the addiction and was released three years into a four-year contract.

"Something has always defined my belief system," he says, when I ask him about religion. And I ask him about religion based on the subtitle of his forthcoming book (now released), called *My Dirty Little Secrets: Steroids, Alcohol, and God.* The book, he says, will be part addiction and recovery, and part sports with an emphasis on the former. It won't, he says, be a Canseco-esque name-naming slash-and-burn piece.

This is a good place to admit that I'm not even sure if Tony Mandarich is a Christian, and am less sure after our conversation. But I very much admire his willingness to take responsibility for his actions, and the steps he took to rectify those mistakes. It's also a good place to assert my belief that Christian sportswriters can write about non-Christian athletes in a way that still upholds the gospel and makes people think about Christ.

"I was born and raised Catholic and don't practice any religion, pardon the pun, *religiously* today," he says. "I always believed in a punishing God, and after all the nonsense I did, I should have been in hell. In fact, I felt like I was in hell. A living hell, day to day."

What I fail to tell him during the interview, but should have, is that we all deserve hell. We've all sinned and fallen short of the glory of God (Romans 3:23), whether we squandered our status as NFL draft choices or our failures have been more private. I should have told him that, in a sense, we do serve a punishing God. God does, in fact, judge. The winnowing fork is in His hand. He separates wheat from chaff. However, He also sent His Son, Jesus, to pay the ultimate penalty for our sinfulness—whether years of drug addiction, unchecked pride, or the heart-level rebellion that's inside all of us. And it's only our acceptance of that payment that renders us clean and justified before Him. Still, Mandarich talks of addiction as the impetus that drove him to explore his faith, and drove him to a sort of rock-bottom humility.

TIME TO MAKE AMENDS— AND A COMEBACK?

"Up until that point I had never hit my knees and asked God for help. I had literally tried thousands of ways to get sober," says Mandarich, who, at this time, was out of the NFL and floundering. He finally checked himself into rehab in Brighton, Michigan, where he was introduced to Alcoholics Anonymous. Part of the AA process, step 9, is the making of amends. "I realized I had to reengage all of these people I had wronged like my former employer, the Packers, and the fans and the media. But how do you make amends with that many people? My thought was to try a comeback . . . do it clean . . . keep my mouth shut, and try to give it everything I had."

The problem was that Mandarich was a lean-by-NFL-terms 255 pounds at the end of rehab. This in the era in which a 300-pound tackle was considered a little light. At 255 Mandarich would have proverbial NFL sand kicked in his face—and that's if he even got an opportunity.

"I realized there was a good chance that nobody would give me a chance," he says. Mandarich worked out for the Indianapolis Colts, where he played from 1996–98, and found a home there, initially on special teams and ultimately in the starting lineup. Finally he was a bona fide NFL tackle and was doing it the right way.

In the 1989 *SI* article, Mandarich claimed to want to be "multifaceted and famous." "Why can't I do what Arnold [Schwartzenegger] did? Bodybuilding. Movies. All of it. I want to be Cyborg III."

Mandarich actually did none of those things, and barely did the one thing he was supposed to do, which is playing left tackle on the professional level. Perhaps more than any athlete before or since, Tony Mandarich rode the roller coaster of human experience. He knew great success, and he knew crushing failure, emptiness, and fear. Like Tom Brady in the previous chapter, he would have a lot in common with the teacher in Ecclesiastes.

Today he is thoughtful and soft-spoken, and is probably blessed to be leading a life as regular as the one he leads in Phoenix, where he runs an Internet marketing firm. He reminds me that perhaps the greatest thing about fame is getting the perspective of people who are past wanting to be famous. Like all ex-ballplayers, though, the pull to compete again is strong. In the midst of all of the tattoos, the Guns N' Roses junk, and the bodybuilding, it's easy to forget that Mandarich also loved playing football.

"I was watching the Colts playoff game the other day," he says. "And I got goose bumps during the national anthem. I told my wife I was sure I could go out and play at least the first series.

"I loved it in Indianapolis," he says. "I loved what I did every day! I was seeing the world through clear eyes again, and doing my dream job. Living with addiction is like living in a fog, but I was like a kid in a candy store in Indianapolis. It felt great to earn my money instead of stealing it."

And then Tony Mandarich laughs out loud.

NOTES

1. I know, two gun references. Freud would have a field day with the 1980s rock landscape.

2. More on that later, but suffice it to say, for now, that I don't believe Mandarich was a bust.

3. I've never been comfortable with the level of glee with which sports columnists talk about draft busts. It's no coincidence that these are usually the talking head types, with no significant sports experiences of their own, who feel personally affronted when athletes fail to live up to expectations.

8

A
REFLECTION

WHEN BAD FANTASY TEAMS
HAPPEN TO GOOD PEOPLE

If winning isn't everything, why do they keep score?

VINCE LOMBARDI
Green Bay Packers coach

osing in your fantasy football playoffs is like being paroled from prison. Or so I tell myself, at about 7:20 p.m. on a Sunday night. Like many Michigan afternoons in December, we received a huge amount of snow, and I spent the first part of the day shoveling my drive and complaining about how impassable the road in front of my house looked. I then spent the rest of the afternoon watching the Lions play a great game of high school football against the professional San Diego Chargers. They lost 51-14. I think Lionel "Little Train" James scored a touchdown or two for the Chargers.

I also had plenty of time to watch my fantasy team, the Rusty Hilgers, lose in the playoffs and write my last fantasy column for PhilSteele.com. The Hilgers lost courtesy of some famously bad performances by players like Rudi Johnson (7 carries, 16 yards, thank you), and Joey Galloway (1 catch, 7 yards). I marveled at how Tampa managed to generate 37 points without in any way involving the speedy and ageless Galloway, who is usually good for a touchdown, according to my exhaustive statistical research. I watched Steve Smith not score for what seemed like the millionth straight week as Carolina started my unemployed next-door neighbor, Matt Moore, at quarterback. I seethed. I seethed like I always seethe, on the Sabbath, when my Rusty Hilgers take one on the chin.

YEAH, A SORE LOSER

My wife knows the telltale signs well. I spend the afternoon in my office, hitting "refresh." My son could be stealing my car, while I mutter things like "I can't believe Anthony Gonzalez chose today to have the game of his life." I knew I had a problem when I typed the following four blurbs in my "Fantasy Duds" column:

Thomas Jones, RB, Jets: 9 carries, plus 19 yards = 1 unemployed journeyman back at the end of the season.

Kevin Jones, RB, Lions: Back to normal with 5 carries for 16 yards. Wow, I'm really getting jaded and cynical about this stuff . . . I should talk to someone.

Rudi Johnson, RB, Bengals: Ahh, Rudi gets back on track with another scintillating 7 carry, 16 yard, no touchdown performance. Note to fantasy owners: It looks like Rudi's off-season started a couple of weeks ago . . .

Joseph Addai, RB, Colts: Makes total sense that he would lay an egg against an Oakland defense that couldn't stop your mom. (See: taking the week off, above . . . see also: I have full-blown anger issues now.)

Lots of people out there are like me—we shouldn't be playing fantasy football. We're called sore losers. That's when I saw the blessing in disguise, which is losing in the fantasy playoffs. I feel it every year that I don't win my league. It's a new lease on life, to overuse an overused cliché. It's like Jason Kidd waking up and realizing he no longer plays for the Nets. Like Isiah Thomas waking up and realizing that nothing after the mid 1980s really happened and that it's all been a bad dream since then.

I get to be a real fan again. I get to be indignant about athletes using drugs so that I can pretend to somehow be morally superior, instead of getting indignant because their suspension will ruin my fantasy season (big public thanks to Travis Henry's legal team here, by the way). I can stop living vicariously through twenty-year-olds. I can vow to never play fantasy again, and break that vow in a few months when training camp starts. (See: "letting your yes be yes"; this is a problem for me.) But the vow feels good today.

I'd also like to take this opportunity to apologize to all of the fine NFL players who I ripped in my fantasy column in 2007. I know you're all reasonably decent kids, many of whom almost got college degrees. I know you try really hard. So let this apology be a comfort to you, along with the millions of dollars sitting in your offshore bank accounts, your luxury automobiles, the Brinks home security systems, and the scads of groupies waiting for you after each game.

But all that to say, I'm glad to not be playing fantasy next week. I'll get to be disappointed at the whole of the Chicago Bears, not just individual players. I get to not spend my week listening to fantasy podcasts and reading Bench/Start lists posted on obscure websites that will probably give my computer a virus. And finally, I'll get to stop referring to Tom Brady as a "fantasy stud" in print, which was starting to feel really awkward for me, if not for Tom too.

Fantasy football, by way of definition, is a game in which points are accrued corresponding to the actual performance of actual players drafted by actual owners. For example, if I have LaDainian Tomlinson on my team and he scores two touchdowns, I'll get twelve points. Probably more for the yardage he accrues. On the flip side, if I draft Vince Young and he throws his customary two interceptions and fails to top a hundred yards, I'll probably be penalized points, maybe even scoring in the negative. At the end of the weekend, the owner with the most points wins his weekly matchup, and just like in real football, the guy with the most wins gets the best playoff seeding and may progress to the championship game.

A handful of disjointed thoughts about fantasy football:

1. *It's **very addictive.*** The amount of time spent by American office workers on fantasy football can't be quantified.[1] I used to be one of these office workers, and spent an inordinate amount of time on it. According to the seventh commandment, it got so bad that I was probably stealing from my employer.

2. *It's probably ruined television coverage of pro football forever.* Those annoying, omnipresent statistical boxes and graphs you see on your Sunday broadcast are the direct result of fantasy football's ascension in popularity. Plus, we have to hear old-timers like Bob Costas try to thinly veil their red-hot hatred for fantasy football while at the same time saying things like "fantasy owners should think about starting Tom Brady this weekend." This is more than a little funny.

3. *Fantasy football has probably ruined traditional "fandom" forever.* I am a Bears fan, but unfortunately it's been a long time since the Bears have had anyone[2] on their roster with anything

resembling "fantasy value."[3] So instead of drafting Bears, I draft guys from other teams, which forces me, sometimes, to root against my Bears on Sunday. For example, if the Bears are playing the Tampa Bay Bucs and Jeff Garcia (I have Garcia), then I'm put in the weird position of hoping he scores several long TDs against the team of my youth. Weird.

4. *Draft Day is really the only fun day*[4] *in fantasy football.* You buy magazines for it. You banter about it for weeks beforehand on e-mail and instant messaging. You go to great lengths to plan the draft on a night and time when every owner can be involved, which means you probably end up having your draft from 11 p.m. to 3 a.m. on a Tuesday night/Wednesday morning. You go to more great lengths to set up your draft online, but run into the inevitable technical difficulties, which means your 11 p.m. draft actually starts at 11:45.

5. *Your wife, if you're married, went to bed an hour ago.* You're surrounded in your home office by magazines[5] and little scraps of paper that say things like "Devard Darling—sleeper"[6] and "draft Eddie Kennison late."[7] You spend an unbelievable amount of time drafting your team. Between picks you banter with other owners on your draft's instant-messaging function. This banter follows one of three threads: "Your pick is lame," "The draft is too long," or, once in a great while, "Let's make a trade."

6. *Some cool celebrities play fantasy football.* For example, there's Vince Vaughn, Joe and Gavin Maloof, and Meat Loaf.[8]

Fantasy football becomes something of a problem for me whenever I hear the commandment that implores us to "remember the Sabbath and keep it holy." Yes, fantasy football takes up Sundays. Where does holiness intersect with wondering if I can maneuver through the church lobby and get home fast enough to get Laurence Maroney and his injured groin out of my lineup before the televised games begin, because I'm playing my best friend today—and losing to my best friend might be enough to not ruin but at least put a dark cloud over the first two or three days of the following week?

At home I wear a path between my office and the couch in front of the television, where I flip like a fiend between Fox and CBS game coverage. Said game coverage has also become an ADD (Attention Deficit Disorder) sufferer's worst nightmare. The screen is littered with a down and distance indicator, a clock, a permanent scoreboard, and a scrolling ticker with fantasy updates. At any time during any telecast, I can chart, carry by carry, how badly my running backs are performing. I can be reminded that Jay Cutler is on his way to another 90-yard, two-interception performance. Somewhere in the middle of all of these graphics is the actual game, which used to be fun to watch but is now an afterthought. Serious players can purchase packages like *NFL Sunday Ticket*, which allow them to toggle between each and every game on the NFL slate, on a given weekend. In addition, there are games on Sunday night, Monday night, and toward the end of the season, Thursday night.

In the office there is NFL.com, which boasts up-to-the-minute scores and statistics, and a mechanism that allows me to track each and every NFL game with a mouse click. I can see real-time drive charts, updated statistics, and scoring summaries. At the very moment the games conclude, I can read Associated Press recaps and watch an online press conference at which coaches say things like "We really came together as a team today," or "We just didn't do enough to get the job done." It's both fascinating and mind-numbingly boring and pointless at the same time.

What we have done, unwittingly, is to take something fun and escapist (football on television) and turn it into "work" on the Sabbath, by making it more realistic. We've gone to great lengths to make our fantasy league "deep," meaning that in order to survive in our league, one must know the Indianapolis Colts' third tight end and also have a cursory knowledge of all NFL draft choices, since our league is also a "keeper" league.[8] If all of this sounds fairly complicated, it's because it is. It has also made Sunday feel like a workday. In essence, I am like an NFL general manager (minus the high salary), scoping the injury list, and scouring other teams' rosters in search of trade possibilities. I have axes to grind with almost every owner in the league based on their un-willingness to trade with me at one time or another. It's juvenile beyond belief, but it's also very grown up, if that makes any sense.

WHAT'S RIGHT WITH FANTASY FOOTBALL

Playing out this fantasy is not all bad. Here are two positive out-comes of fantasy football that may counteract everything I wrote in the last section:

1. *Fantasy football gives men something to talk about in the church lobby.* Believe it or not, "How's your fantasy team doing?" is much more "authentic" and helpful than the kind of "How are you?" ... "Fine, how are YOU?" ... "Fine" dialogue that has hap-pened between men in church lobbies since the beginning of church-lobby time.

2. *Fantasy football offers men a mechanism to keep in touch and stay in relationships.* I have probably been in around ten to twelve men's small groups since leaving college, but I have stayed in one fantasy league, where I have seen my co-owners marry and have children, though thankfully never on Draft Day. And in spite of the axes that I grind regarding trades (see above), I have probably grown in my friendships with all of them and consider myself lucky to actually have friends, because most Christian men don't seem to have any.

My wife can sense my bad mood, which started toward the end of the early games. I become sullen and withdrawn. She asks, "What's wrong?" and I say, "Nothing," which of course means that something is wrong. The problem is that the "something" that is wrong is that I lost to my buddy, aka Team Stache, in fantasy this Sunday. Peyton Manning has one bad game per season, generally, and he chose today to have that bad game. Subsequently, my buddy picked an overweight running back named DeShawn Wynn off the waiver wire who was previously mired as low as fourth on the Green Bay Packers depth chart. Today, however, he rushed for 100 yards and a score. I'm inconsolable.

I'm upset because I'm the "Football Guy." I'm also a professional sportswriter with a weekly fantasy column. I'm supposed to know about this stuff. Therefore, I feel that it is not only my right but also my expectation to win every fantasy game on the schedule by a healthy margin. For very ridiculous reasons, I'm finding my identity in all of this.

I pout from room to room, and slump into the passenger's seat of our car, figuring that evening church will be better than sitting through the 4:30 games. During the hymn sing I mouth the words to *Lift High the Cross,* but I'm really trying to figure out why I didn't see the DeShawn Wynn thing coming. I mean, I have his backfield mate—Brandon Jackson —on my roster. Jackson was supposed to be the starter. Not Wynn.

REAL FOOTBALL

I remember my first real, live NFL game. My parents took me to see the Indianapolis Colts in 1984, the first year the Colts were in town after packing a truck and leaving Baltimore[9] under the veil of night. The game took place in the Hoosier Dome, since renamed the RCA Dome, and since (2008) rebuilt as Lucas Oil Stadium—double the size of the

Dome. I have seen the life cycle of a pro stadium. This makes me feel profoundly old.

I was eight years old when the Colts arrived in Indy, and the NFL was like a Disney-esque dream world to me. I wanted, more than anything in life, to be an NFL player, but for now, just being under the same roof, breathing the same recycled air, and being able to walk past the gates and gaze down upon the Crayola-green Astroturf was more than enough. Unbeknownst to me, this would be the first of many games— NFL, Big Ten, MAC, and small college—that I would have the privilege of enjoying with my father. When he dies people will talk about what a nice guy Ted Kluck Sr. was—spiritual leader, great pilot, all that stuff—but I will remember the games we shared together.

Each game Dad and I attended was filled with talk—about the players, the coaches, and about the plays and being able to see them develop from up high. Even though we were Colts fans, we rarely cheered for a team on those days, rather, we were "just happy to be there." And we were happy to be there, together, watching football. Watching tackles, dropped passes, interceptions, and long runs. We were even happy watching the Colts lose, which they did often in those days. We lost ourselves in those games, and as much as it was a dream world for me, it was escapism for him.

I hope as my own sons grow older, this is how we'll watch football together—if he even wants to watch it at all. I hope I don't waste those moments kvetching about Edgerrin James not getting enough carries, or Bill Belichick never releasing his injury reports. I hope I've moved on. I hope there's something beyond fantasy football and I hope that particular "something" is that it goes away completely.

The Colts played the Houston Oilers (now the Tennessee Titans) that night in the Hoosier Dome, in what cynics call a "meaningless" preseason game. The Oilers were quarterbacked by Warren Moon, who is now in the Pro Football Hall of Fame. The Colts would finish 4–12 that year and were quarterbacked, in part, by Art Schlichter, who would do time for gambling-related incidents—all of which was unbeknownst to me as an eight-year-old. I couldn't tell you who won that night, but I do know that I hyperventilated in the car on the way home. From all the excitement.

An Aside on David Mamet and Mixed Martial Arts

We can learn a lot from the worlds of fantasy football and real football. But we can also learn much about life from the curious world of mixed martial arts (MMA). I recently read an article in *World* magazine[10] on the "outing" of playwright/screenwriter David Mamet—an MMA fan—as a conservative. Mamet, a bespectacled little baby-boomer, is responsible for great movies like *Wag the Dog* and *Glengarry Glen Ross* among others. Mamet has written fiction, essays, a great book on acting, children's stories, and television commercials. He's a player. So not surprisingly, his announcement sent shockwaves through the traditionally liberal arts-and-letters community.

Mamet wrote an essay in *The Village Voice*, itself a bastion of liberality, entitled: "Why I'm No Longer a Brain-Dead Liberal." In a (very small) nutshell, Mamet suggests that his presuppositions about liberalism—that government is corrupt, business is exploitative, and people are really good at heart—are all wrong. Especially the last one, which is especially interesting given that most of his movies deal exclusively with bad people.

The article chose not to mention Mamet's longtime involvement in mixed martial arts or MMA. The playwright has trained for six years in a Brazilian Jiu Jitsu academy in Los Angeles and is, according to an ESPN.com report, fiercely loyal to his gym and his trainer. He has made a movie, *Redbelt*, about

MMA, which has been billed as "a love letter" to his gym. Why do I mention this, especially in conjunction with Mamet's outing as a conservative?

I think MMA, at some level, may have something to do with Mamet's conservatism because it (fighting) is perhaps the most capitalistic thing ever invented by man. If you win fights, you get more money. It's that simple. If you train harder, and longer, than your opponents, you will probably win more fights. It's individual. It's entrepreneurial. So for Mamet to embrace this world, especially after spending most of his life in a liberal, socialist enclave like the arts, is significant.

I have an odd fascination with mixed martial arts. If you're not familiar with the sport, it also goes by the unofficial moniker of "cage fighting." That's right: two guys in an octagonal cage, trying to beat each other up. A fighter can win a match by decision if it goes the distance (rare), or by knocking out your opponent (less rare), or by getting him to "tap out" or give up (common).

On the surface, MMA is an aberration, and for many it's a mile marker of our ongoing fall of civilization. I agree with the critics (including Senator John McCain, who is also, oddly, a huge boxing fan) to some degree. MMA has spawned some famously bad reality television shows, and has seemingly given us a generation of young men who walk around trying to look tough, wearing black "Tap Out" T-shirts, goatees, and shaven heads. It's the whole "tough by association" phenomenon.

It has also given us good losers. Like boxers, MMA fighters are a small, close-knit fraternity. There is a huge amount of loyalty within MMA, and the fighters have a great deal of respect for one another. As in other sports, there are Christian participants (most notably nine-time Ultimate Fighting Championships

Welterweight Champion Matt Hughes), and there are now more rules in place to maintain order and protect the participants.

I'm not sure whether it's okay for Christians to watch MMA, and while I have watched it in the past and watch it occasionally now, I do so very infrequently. It almost always creeps me out. But that said, its fighters are paragons of self-control. You may wonder how men who fight for money in a cage can embody the biblical concept of self-control, but indeed self-control is, I think, the whole idea of the sport. Like boxers, MMA fighters have been stripped of the luxury of emotional outbursts. Basketball players frequently jaw at referees, football players can dance around on the field and express themselves emotionally, and baseball managers routinely enter into dirt-kicking tantrums on the base paths. Conversely, if a fighter allows himself a split second to whine to the official or engage the fans, he will probably end up concussed (at worst) and a loser. Fighting requires long stretches of unbroken concentration.

It also requires a sort of boring, plodding commitment to a goal. Contrary to popular Christian writing, our faith lives aren't always wildly adventurous and revolutionary. They're often hard and frustrating. There's a sort of plodding commitment involved in prayer, Bible reading, church life, service, and other spiritual disciplines.

I've interviewed MMA fighters and their training lives are remarkably boring. They work on six hundred repetitions of the same roundhouse kick, so that they can throw it in a fight without thinking about it. They run long distances by themselves. They grapple. It's boring, but if they want to have success when it counts, they have to do it. That's why it's a lot easier to buy a "Tap Out" T-shirt than it is to actually be an MMA fighter.

Real fighters don't run around feeling like William Wallace or the Russell Crowe character from *Gladiator*.

Please don't read this as a John Eldredge-ian support of fighting as the new way to be "a man." That would be ridiculous, in every sense of the word "ridiculous." Truthfully, I'd be brokenhearted if my own sweet son wanted to be an MMA fighter. But I do think that it's possible to think Christianly and also learn from the sport.

NOTES

1. Although the actual amount of time devoted to fantasy football can be quantified, *Business Week* reports that more than 15 million U.S. adults play fantasy sports.

2. For what it's worth, it was probably Thomas Jones a couple of years ago or, if you're in a league that allows special teams points, Devin Hester circa 2007.

3. This little bit of jargon strikes me as odd. The fact that grown men assess the "fantasy value" of other grown men seems, at worst, deviant, and, at best, something that they probably should talk about a whole lot.

4. The same feeling is true for the Detroit Lions in real football.

5. There are at least a half dozen "fantasy draft guide" magazines that pop up each summer, each claiming to have "what it takes to help you draft a championship team." All of them, essentially, have the same thing to offer: the opinion of a handful of football fans, just like you. I have no idea why I keep buying these magazines each year, but I do.

6. An obscure wide receiver who started his career with the Baltimore Ravens, did nothing, and is now with the Kansas City Chiefs. Darling is perhaps best known for his brother Devaughn's tragic death during an off-season workout at Florida State University.

7. Eddie Kennison is a mediocre wide receiver who has had a long career with the St. Louis Rams, the Chicago Bears, and, most recently, the Kansas City Chiefs. More importantly though, he is the subject of an ongoing inside joke involving one of my old college buddies, Scott Shortenhaus. I used to call his high-powered Washington, D.C., political office, ask for him, and tell the receptionist that my name was "Eddie Kennison." I even bought him an autographed Eddie Kennison photo as a wedding gift.

8. Meaning owners are allowed to keep a handful of veteran guys each year, plus several "rookies" from that year's incoming class. The result is that I have had Peyton Manning on my roster for several years, but have had a revolving door of rookie keepers.

9. I remember feeling sorry, very briefly, for the children of Baltimore for losing their team. But this sentiment was short-lived and soon replaced by the joy of having their team in my general vicinity.

10. *World* is, in my opinion, one of the few good Christian magazines on the market, precisely because they care enough to write about stuff like this, and do it from an orthodox perspective.

9

SPORTS
and FILM

I'm your huckleberry.

DOC HOLLIDAY
Tombstone

I don't know what it means to be someone's "huckleberry," and I don't think anyone else knows either. It doesn't matter. What matters is that, as Doc Holliday, Val Kilmer delivered that line with copious amounts of swagger and cool, channeling the physicality of Keith Richards, James Dean, Iggy Pop, and Jim Morrison all at the same time. You wanted a friend like Doc Holliday when you saw *Tombstone*. You wanted to be Doc Holliday.

In one of the film's most telling scenes, Holliday, seemingly on his deathbed, hears Wyatt Earp tell him that he (Earp) has no chance of beating his nemesis, the evil Johnny Ringo, in a gun duel. Earp is scheduled to duel with Ringo later that evening and rides off on horseback to, ostensibly, meet his maker. Before doing so, however, he lays his sheriff's badge on Holliday's chest, in a quintessential "male friendship" moment.

Instead, when the film takes us to the location of the duel, there is a man in black, looking cooler smoking a cigarette than perhaps any other man, real or in cinema, has ever looked smoking.[1] It is, of course, Holliday, and he has rallied from tuberculosis to go and fight Ringo himself, exclaiming, "Why, Johnny Ringo, you look like you just saw a ghost."

He then pops Ringo in the forehead, essentially saving his friend's life, and then he and Earp go on to clean out the Cowboys (bad guys) before Earp has one last game of poker with Doc before essentially laying him to rest in a Colorado sanatorium.

Why do I mention this film, and Ringo, when neither seem to have much to do with sports? I mention them, in part, because *Tombstone* was the quintessential "guy" movie of the early to mid 1990s, and was huge with athletes,[2] in part because it showed guys doing the things that we want most to do—being brave, heroic, and cool, and having the right thing to say at the right time. It also portrayed male friendships in a very real way. Even typing the words "male friendships" makes me feel less than masculine (read: like a sissy). It evokes images of counselor types in turtlenecks using words like "intimacy" and "mother complex."

SPORTS BUDDY MOVIES

Still, if you think of almost every successful sports film, there is a significant "buddy" component. Replace the *Tombstone* story line with that of *Rocky IV*, the sucky-but-imminently-watchable one where Rocky travels to Siberia to train for a fight he can't win (which, of course, he does) vs. the steroid-tough Ivan Drago[3] who, by the way, killed Rocky's best friend, Apollo Creed, in the ring in a charity match at the beginning of the movie. Essentially the whole film is a tribute to Rocky's friendship with Creed, and draws heavily from friend footage from their previous three films together. It would feel weird if it wasn't a film that culminated in a bloody, thirty-minute boxing match.

In fact, the whole *Rocky* franchise hits the friendship/heroism thing pretty hard. In addition to Rocky always battling long odds, there is his ever-growing relationship with Mickey Goldmill, the grizzed-but-father-figurish trainer who shares life lessons about women, and how they weaken legs, among other things. In *Rocky II*, Rocky and Creed use the shared experience of beating each other senseless as a springboard to a lifelong friendship. Believe it or not, this happens a lot in sports, where mortal enemies on the field often become best friends off of it.

Consider also the high school football film *Friday Night Lights*, which was based on a classic book by H. G. Bissinger and on which a predictably bad television series was spawned. The film, directed brilliantly by Peter Berg, follows the lives of a handful of high school players at Permian High School in Odessa, Texas. The film is a gritty look at the realities of football worship in Texas—forgotten academics, the illiterate-but-physically brilliant running back who gets hurt, the nasty-but-still-likeable embattled coach, the almost psychotically unbalanced townspeople, etc. But the real story line happens between the players (who are based on real players). There is the son of lawyers, Brian Chavez, who will go on to study at Harvard. There is the son of an abusive alcoholic, Don Billingsly, who wants nothing more than to please a father who doesn't deserve to be pleased. There is quarterback Mike Winchell, who is dealing with the pressures of starting-quarterback-ness, while also caring for his sick mother.

What the boys have in common is that they all play for Permian, they will all lose the state title many bloody hits and hard practices later—and they are all best friends with each other. As the last scene illustrates, the three players will probably remain best friends, despite their differences, for the rest of their lives.

When I was finishing college, in the late 1990s, I had the weird sensation of going to a lot of Christian conferences, and hearing a lot of young Christian guys go on and on about how much they loved the movie *Braveheart*. The film seemed like a paean to Mel Gibson made by his favorite actor, Mel Gibson, yet for some reason it captured the imaginations of a lot of young Christian men who were mired in a pretty wussified evangelical culture.

Imagine a ballroom full of Campus Crusade students at a missions conference, singing their hearts out over flavor-of-the-month praise songs, and then having a couple of leader types come up front to do *Braveheart*-related skits (think one guy in a kilt and lots of fake swords), which drive the crowd wild (in a good way). I've been to good Christian conferences where this has happened, and the juxtaposition was striking—a roomful of pretty privileged, upscale Christian white kids all enraptured by the actions of a Scottish revolutionary/warlord who was known to have dismembered the bodies of his enemies after slaying them in battle.

Christians lit on the whole idea of one-man-sacrificing-for-many, and decided that *Braveheart*, in spite of its classic Hollywood revenge ethic, was suitable Christian man fare. I'm not saying there's anything wrong with this, only that it's interesting that young, Christian men seemed a little too eager to devour and want to relive the film. In addition to the Gibson character's handiness with the sword—William Wallace seemed to have killed about 1,200 people on his own in the film, all in uniquely bloody ways that made him look more and more awesome—he also gained the respect of his countrymen, was beloved by his soldiers, and had a better-than-average friendship with the film's only source of comic relief, a big, red-haired Scottish oaf named Hamish.

KNEE-DEEP IN *BRAVEHEART* MANIA

In the interest of fairness, I think I'm one of about three men in the world who didn't care for *Braveheart*. Believe it or not, this created a little bit of awkwardness for me at the time. I got a lot of "what are you, gay?" looks from other young, Christian men who were knee-deep in *Braveheart* mania. My theory at the time was that if someone is an athlete (I was), he is, in essence, living the movie. He and his teammates are doing hard things together. They are probably, at some level, surviving a tyrant (coach), overcoming great obstacles (injuries, losses, etc.), and forming inseparable, lifetime, Hamish-like bonds with each other. So when you're living it, a movie like *Braveheart* becomes infinitely less fascinating.

Chariots of Fire is considered by many to be the only decent "Christian" movie ever made, and its makers have gone to great lengths to explain that it wasn't supposed to be explicitly "Christian." What the film was, undoubtedly, was a beautiful character study on many of the most basic elements of manhood. Success. Failure. Legacy. Race. Acceptance. Love. It did all of this in a very understated, artistic way, that makes me wonder how Christians who loved *Chariots* can also be wild about *Braveheart*, which to me seemed like the cinematic equivalent of a blunt club to the temple.

And I think we probably have movies like *Braveheart* to thank for books like *Wild at Heart* that reduce Christian man-ness to an adventure that often involves being outside and hiking around, pretending that we are someone like William Wallace.

This all begs the question: Why is the world so good at making movies that portray compassion, self-sacrifice, heroism, and cool know-what-to-say-in-the-heat-of-battle male friendships, but we (Christians) excel at making lame movies about these things?

A new Hollywood subculture is afoot, surrounding the ideas, futures, and careers of the heretofore nonexistent (Ralph Winter and Tom Shadyac aside) "Christian" filmmaker. There are websites and books devoted to Christian filmmakers, and speakers tours in which aspiring young filmmakers can pay big dollars to hear other aspiring Christian filmmakers speak who have never actually made films that anyone has watched or would potentially want to watch.

There are five key elements that secular movies have that Christian moviegoers want in films on sports.

First, we want father figures. We see this with the Gene Hackman character in *Hoosiers*, the Denzel Washington character in *Remember the Titans*, the Mickey the trainer (Burgess Meredith) character in *Rocky*, and even the Reggie Dunlop (Paul Newman) character in *SlapShot*. We're a culture that seems to be obsessed with a certain kind of father figure—tough but compassionate; wry and sarcastic but not so wry and sarcastic as to not be loving; successful; charismatic; and real. And perhaps it is because no father can be all of these things all the time, that these film embodiments are so very appealing.

The relationship between Harold Abrahams in *Chariots of Fire* and his coach, Sam Mussabini, is especially poignant. Abrahams is so driven toward victory that he can't get close to anyone except his coach, who in addition to driving him toward victory also becomes his only true friend. Abrahams is alone, in a dark pub, with Mussabini after he finally wins the gold medal in the 100-meter dash, and they have the quintessential "Is this all there is?" moment together. It is profoundly sad, but at least they have each other.

Second, Christian moviegoers want heroes (and an enemy to triumph over). In *Rocky IV* (which, as mentioned earlier, is my favorite terrible movie of all time), a rapidly aging but unbelievably ripped

Rocky Balboa takes on the unbeatable, roided-up Russian giant Ivan Drago to avenge his friend's death. But before doing so he trains hard—running through six feet of snow with a tree trunk across his shoulders, doing sit-ups from the rafters of his kibbutz in the Russian countryside, even lifting rocks. He also fixes a babushka's broken wagon and yells "Adrian" from the top of a mountain. More importantly, he rallies in the ring to beat Drago, while at the same time impressing his son's friends and winning over Drago's entire Russian fan base, including a politician with a birthmark on his forehead that's supposed to be Mikhael Gorbachev. He then gives a speech (everybody can change—classic) that brings the Cold War to an end in one fell swoop.

Sometimes, in cinema, the hero stories are real, as in the case of *Miracle* (about the 1980 USA hockey triumph in the Olympics) and *Hoosiers* (about Indiana high school basketball). Both movies involve ragtag bunches of underdogs who come together for a common purpose and vanquish a swaggering, arrogant, seemingly unbeatable opponent. There is satisfaction to be found in the coming together element, but also in the smack-down appeal of seeing a jerky opponent get handed his lunch. We're not above this as Christians (see also: David and Goliath).

Third, Christian moviegoers want single-mindedness. Part of the appeal of the *Rocky* movies (there were six in the franchise) is that Rocky seemed to care about only two things in life—beating whoever was in front of him at the time, and his wife, Adrian. This is appealing on both an athletic and a romantic level. His life seemed stripped of many of the complications that we experience. When he was training—doing one-armed push-ups, drinking egg yolks, running, and hitting the punching bag (and, in *Rocky III*, even racing and then frolicking in the surf with Apollo in one of the worst scenes in American cinema)—he seemed to want for nothing except victory.

This singleness of purpose is something that Christian guys long

THE REASON FOR SPORTS

for but rarely achieve in our spiritual lives. For me, I know that I'm involved in the single most important, relevant, and interesting thing in the history of mankind—the gospel—but why then am I so much more interested in winning my pickup game at the "Y" or making sure my fantasy football team goes undefeated? Why do I admire Rocky's passion so much that I get chills every time I hear the theme music from the *Rocky* training montage?

Fourth, Christian moviegoers want friendships. Generally, two types of friendships dominate sports movies. There's the socially conscious, you're-supposed-to-learn-something-about-society type of friendships, which include Brian Piccolo and Gale Sayers in the TV movie *Brian's Song*, and Coach Boone and his players in *Remember the Titans*. Racial divides are crossed, things are learned, and the friendships onscreen often tower over anything we've ever experienced in real life.

The second type is the united-in-a-common-cause-against-our-opponents friendships. These include Frodo and Sam in the *Lord of the Rings* trilogy (okay, it's not sports), and the guys in *Breaking Away*[4] who are united not only by their lack of money (they're townies) but also in their desire to defeat the evil frat kids in the film's climactic bicycle race.

Fifth, violence, with a caveat. Why is it that Christians are okay with watching *Band of Brothers* and seeing American soldiers routinely blowing up foreigners, or *Rocky IV* in which Rocky lands countless, blood-inducing blows to the face of Ivan Drago, but are uncomfortable watching Jake LaMotta carve up pretty boy Tony Janiro[5] in *Raging Bull*. Both are instances of staged, cinematic boxing violence, but one has violence with a noble purpose (beating up an evil Russian, see above) but one just seems sadistic and wrong.

Christians are almost unanimous in their support of *Braveheart* and the *Lord of the Rings* movies, which both feature hours-worth of poorly lit, thousands-of-lives-lost epic battle scenes where good and evil supposedly hang in the balance; but they're quick to decry film violence in other situations.

So why is it that Christians make such weak sports movies? They simplify how God acts and prayer works. They have simple characters and trite dialogue and—dare we say it—mediocre acting. One example is *Facing the Giants*, which follows the fortunes of Coach Grant Taylor at Shiloh Christian Academy[6]—a school that has never had a winning season. Grant, it turns out, has a myriad of other problems besides his soft football team—his car is constantly on the fritz (say it ain't so!), and he and his wife are infertile, which adds a weirdly heavy element to the entire proceeding.

The awkwardly heavy-handed message in this film is that prayer does things. Specifically, prayer makes your previously soft, weak team good overnight, it allows your noodle-legged field goal kicker with the paraplegic father (tug heartstrings here) to drill a 51-yarder to win state, it gets you a new car, and it allows you and your wife to have a child.

These are all good things that I'm glad happened to earnest Coach Grant Taylor, but they are, I think, a gross misrepresentation of prayer and the gospel. After Taylor wins the Big Game, he receives word from his wife that he has made another team, the "daddy team," which is, if not the single worst line of dialogue in film history, certainly up there. There are plenty of good Christian coaches who, in God's sovereignty, still lose. There are countless praying couples who can't conceive. God gives and takes away, in His sovereignty, but *Giants* made it seem like Coach T prayed his way into fertility and a running game.

The other glaring problem with *Giants* is that there were already two good, family-friendly football movies in *Rudy* and *Remember the Titans* on the market, made with professional actors and a Hollywood budget. Beyond their sound production values, both contained the same soaring, inspirational happy endings and, better yet, were true stories. We needed *Facing the Giants* like we need a basketball movie about a small, Christian high school in Indiana that hires a controversial coach, starts praying, signs a stud homeschooler, and then wins state. That movie, *Hoosiers*, has already been done, minus the praying.

WHAT *CHARIOTS OF FIRE* DOES RIGHT

Chariots of Fire works because it so effortlessly contains many of the elements I wrote about above—friendship, single-mindedness, heroes, and father figures—and does so in a professional, nonpreachy but nevertheless forthright way. Here are four other elements present in *Chariots of Fire* (winner of the best picture Academy Award in 1981).

First, male issues. At its heart, *Chariots* is a movie about what it means to be a man. Does being successful make you a man, as Harold Abrahams would have you believe? Is it wealth and a carefree life that make you a man, as is the case for Lord Lindsay? What of the loser, the man who at the end of the day doesn't have what it takes to get the job done, as portrayed by the humble and kind Aubrey Montague? Or is it standing up for the gospel, like Eric Liddell, when actual important things are at stake?

It didn't cost Coach Taylor in *Facing the Giants* anything to begin praying when his team was mired in a losing slide. His risks were not great, and his solution pretty easy—just pray (along with tinker with the lineup, wear your lucky socks, and adjust practice times). But Liddell had much more to lose—his reputation, his team's respect, and a chance to compete for a gold medal. He also had a much greater challenge—to honor God at the risk of not running when his country said he must.

Second, layered characters. Harold Abrahams is more than a type-A, driven sprinter hell-bent on a gold medal. He's also a young man coming to grips with his ethnic Judaism in a culture that he feels is set on his marginalization. He is trying to have a relationship with a woman who doesn't need his fame and doesn't understand his life's work. His best friend, Montague, is a sanguine soul. He provides comfort and a nonjudgmental listening ear for Abrahams, though their religions and background differ greatly. At one point Abrahams compliments his friend, calling him "his most complete man. You're brave, compassionate, kind: a content man. That is your secret, contentment; I am twenty-four and I've never known it."

Eric Liddell struggles with his desire to compete, when his sister wants him to commit his life to the foreign mission field, and ultimately has to decide between the grandeur of the Olympics, and his convictions about competing on Sunday. And perhaps my favorite character in the film, Lord Andrew Lindsay, puts aside his unbridled hedonism[7] to sacrifice his place in a race so that Liddell can run.

Third, competition (including both winning and losing). The directors of *Chariots* accurately captured the tension, excitement, and at times unbridled joy that comes from competing. The directors of the film intentionally shot the final 100-meter dash in real time, meaning that it took roughly ten seconds on-screen to show the finality, and the "here and gone" element of Olympic glory (see: Abrahams on justifying his existence). They capture what it feels like to be young and fast, but they also capture what it's like to be young and not fast enough, as the film's most important moments come when Harold Abrahams loses.

When Abrahams explains, before the race, that he has "ten seconds to justify my existence," we can relate. An author may feel that he has one great book to justify his writer's existence and to feed his family. Or a childless woman may feel as though one child would justify her existence. The examples go on and on. Abrahams is often painted as a villain, but he is a pretty accurate portrait of all Christians who struggle to be happy and holy in Jesus. And so he reminds us of our need to determine what is important to living and what gives purpose and peace to our earthly existence.

Fourth, the gospel. Eric Liddell explains that when he runs, he "feels God's pleasure." That outpouring of joy over the grace of God and His forgiveness manifests itself in Liddell's commitment to his sport, but also in the light grip with which he holds his sport and competition, and his willingness to give it all away for the sake of the cross.

Liddell, who would later die in a concentration camp, explains that unlike Coach Taylor's gospel in *Giants*, the Christian life isn't all blue ribbons and new cars; instead, the Scotsman echoes the apostle Paul when he says, "I want to compare faith to running in a race. It's hard. It requires concentration of will, energy of soul."

What's sometimes lost in striving for the gospel and depicting truth in sports movies is that we happen to be involved in what we know is the greatest underdog-makes-good story in the history of mankind. The gospel. In fact, our underdog was so underdog that He died on a cross like a common criminal, willingly, of course, to pay the penalty for our many sins. Not so that if we pray, we can magically have something in return—receive a new car, stop the spread of communism, win the state title, or even have a baby.

People will keep making sports movies, and I'll keep watching them, both good and bad.[8] But in the meantime, I want to publicly thank the makers of *Chariots of Fire* who crafted a film that managed to lift high the cross, make us think, entertain us, and didn't cause us to be embarrassed to use the words "Christian" and "film" in the same sentence.

NOTES

1. Besides James Dean, who is the undisputed king of looking cool while smoking a ciggy.

2. The Christian college football team I played briefly for at Taylor University had T-shirts made emblazoned with a quote from the movie: "It's not revenge, it's a reckoning."

3. Portrayed brilliantly by the great Dolph Lundgren, who gave us such lines as "I must break you" and "He's like a piece of iron." Most of the guys I went to college with can pretty much recite this film verbatim.

4. If you're ever in the mood to watch a bicycling movie (is that anyone?), it should be this one, which is an underrated gem of a sports movie. And it stars the guy who played American sprinter Charlie Paddock in *Chariots of Fire*.

5. *Raging Bull* is one of the most beautifully shot films in all of American cinema, and the scene I'm referring to concerns the wildly jealous LaMotta, and the fact that his wife makes an offhand comment about his upcoming opponent, Janiro, being attractive. Fueled by his jealousy, LaMotta not only beats Janiro but does so savagely, as to prove to his wife who is the bigger man. The scene is extremely uncomfortable, as is the entire movie, which I can't in good conscience recommend but still think is amazing.

6. If this had been real life, Coach Taylor would have found a deep-pocketed donor at Shiloh who could have visited the Big City and lured away a running back from Booker T. Washington High, who would have single-handedly rushed his ball club to the state title. Instead he prayed once and that worked too.

7. I love the scene where Lindsay practices hurdling with a glass of champagne perched atop each hurdle.

8. In the interest of honesty, I have to admit that I've watched, and liked, bad sports movies including *The Program*, *Major League*, and *Any Given Sunday*.

10

SPORTS
and SEXUALITY

WHY THE NFL SCOUTING COMBINE AND VIAGRA COMMERCIALS MAKE ME FEEL LIKE A PIECE OF MEAT

A short sprint is run on nerves. It's tailor-made for neurotics.

SAM MUSSABINI
Chariots of Fire

A short sprint "is tailor-made for neurotics," Coach Sam Mussabini
tells Harold Abrahams. A short sprint is also tailor-made for television. It's perfect for our miniscule American attention spans. We get to
see a winner and a loser, over the short span of a few seconds. We get
to see muscular bodies moving in unison.

The NFL Scouting Combine is the new Olympics, and its 40-yard
dash is the new 100-meter dash. For those unfamiliar, the combine is
the NFL's annual scouting meat market at which three hundred or so
of the most physically promising college seniors are gathered in Indianapolis, where they are stripped, poked, prodded, weighed, measured,
ogled, blogged about, talked about, and psychologically evaluated by
each of the NFL's thirty-two teams and their armies of talent evaluators. Teams do this, of course, because they're investing huge amounts

of money on these players. The lowest paid among this lot will still make upwards of $300,000, and the first rounders will command multimillions.

For football coaches and GMs, the annual event (formally called the National Invitational Camp) is equivalent to test-driving a car before you buy it. It's damage control. The good part is, unlike the Olympics, the marquee event happens three hundred times (once for each player) and invited guests and a national audience (on the NFL Network) don't have to sit through Bob Costas, human interest features, or rhythmic gymnastics to get to it.

I say that the combine is the new Olympics because it is a well-packaged, made-for-television event that showcases the most capitalistic of capitalist pursuits—young men running after money. I wrote in another book, *Game Time*, that it would make Ayn Rand drool. This is an event where a tenth of a second in the 40-yard dash can cost a kid millions. So he's not only running for himself, he's running for his momma, his daddy, his cousins, his grandma, and his children's children. This is a big deal.

THOSE NFL MISTAKES

Still, the NFL makes mistakes. It's rare that the NFL's roving band of talent evaluators, who fall in their duties somewhere between grizzled old football vagabonds and FBI operatives, would all need to take a mulligan in the same year. The year of our Lord, 1991, was just such a year. The first round is littered with names like Bruce Pickens, Charles McRae, Antone Davis, Stan Thomas, and Huey Richardson. Never heard of these players? It's because they made hardly a ripple in the waters of NFL history but were all highly paid, highly sought-after first-round draft picks.

The first round of the 1991 draft yielded exactly zero players who will be in the Hall of Fame, as compared to 1990, a first round that produced (in order of my perceived importance) Emmitt Smith, Junior Seau, Cortez Kennedy, and Richmond Webb in the elite star category, as well as solid players such as Mark Carrier, Lamar Lathon, Tony Bennett (the linebacker, not the crooner), and Rodney Hampton.

Even 1992, considered to be another weak first round, produced longtime multiple Pro Bowlers like Troy Vincent and Ray Roberts, a Super Bowl MVP in Desmond Howard, the recipient of one of the more famous (or infamous) free-agent deals in league history in Sean Gilbert, and longtime starters including Robert Porcher, John Fina, Chester McGlockton, Terrell Buckley, Marco Coleman, and Bob Whitfield.

This is significant because the NFL would like you to think that it makes very few mistakes, the Detroit Lions notwithstanding, when it comes to player evaluation. But the 1991 first round is a black hole in league history. Why? Because, with a few exceptions, everyone stunk at the same time. The round produced only seven players who appeared in Pro Bowls, and of those players only Ted Washington and perhaps Herman Moore could be considered elite at their positions.

The NFL has also hopped into bed (sorry, pun intended) with the scores of erectile dysfunction pill producers, including but not limited to Enzyte, Viagra, and Cialis, who advertise nonstop during NFL television events. This creates the impression that NFL fans do nothing but drink ice-cold, frost-brewed Coors Light, drive huge two-ton extended-cab Hemi-powered Dodge Ram trucks, and struggle with sexual performance. This is a disturbing image indeed.

Sex and sports have always gone hand in hand. Ring card girls cavorting, nearly naked, between rounds at boxing matches. NFL cheerleaders, also nearly naked, cavorting during television timeouts. "Broadway" Joe Namath, wearing BeautyMist nylons in an advertisement, and generally flaunting his appealing-ness to both women (who want to be with him) and men (who want to be him). The annual *Sports Illustrated* swimsuit issue that has been hidden by parents and snuck by teenagers is going on three generations now. Many fans have long been fascinated by these Bunyanesque (Paul not John) characters for their actions on the field (athletic) and off it (sexual). See also Babe Ruth, Mike Tyson, and Wilt Chamberlain. Christians are outwardly, and rightfully, disgusted by their actions but a little part of us, too, is amazed by them.

Sports are about the celebration of physical prowess, among other things. Watching a broad-shouldered, 265-pound linebacker with 3 percent body fat cover forty yards in 4.5 seconds is exciting in large part because it's something we can't do ourselves. It's attractive. Ditto for watching Michael Jordan soar from the free throw line or Tony Hawk hitting a 900 skateboard trick on a vert ramp. These actions are breathtaking because of the sheer audacity and physical prowess it takes to pull them off.

PRODUCTS TO MAKE US FASTER, STRONGER, AND SEXUALLY POTENT

Is it any surprise, then, that advertisers try to catch us at our most vulnerable, to sell us products we don't need? They hawk products that might make us bigger, faster, and stronger (sports equipment), products that will make us feel bigger (huge trucks), and even make us more sexually potent.

Even our sports news is infused with sexuality. As I write this, the morning sports headlines include a piece on whether married NBA basketball star Dwayne Wade is having an affair with forty-six-year-old Star Jones, who is also cohost of *The View*.[1] Another headline speculates as to whether baseball icon Roger Clemens had an affair with a fifteen-year-old country musician. This after a piece that speculated on Clemens's supposed tryst with golfer John Daly's wife. Who needs the gossip columns when we have ESPN.com?

Call me old school, but I liked it a lot better when I didn't know everything about the sexual peccadilloes of all of my favorite athletes. I liked it better when kids could talk about Roger Clemens's fastball, not the number of aspiring music starlets he did or didn't bed. But as everyone knows, sex sells. It gets ratings. And let's face it, it's interesting. I'm not going to try to convince you that sex is boring. It's anything but. I'm just saying that sports were more interesting, and more fun, without it.

As a married man and a Christian, it makes me sad when I hear about athletes' failing marriages, or athletes who are publicly unfaithful to their wives or husbands. There is no "I told you so" or "look how immoral this person is" satisfaction in seeing that news. It's sad. It should be heartbreaking.

I liked it better when I didn't have to explain (or rather dance around) the term "erectile dysfunction" to my son, or try to gently explain to him why Bob is smiling so much in the Enzyte commercials. And what to make of heroes? When I was a kid I didn't know whether a certain athlete was unfaithful to his wife. It didn't cross my mind to think of such things. I wanted to see him do something spectacular, and I wanted to do it too. That's all I knew.

Finally, brothers, whatever is true, whatever is noble, whatever is right, whatever is pure, whatever is lovely, whatever is admirable—if anything is excellent or praiseworthy—think about such things.

Philippians 4:8

So what do we do with this, as Christians? Do we add sports to an already monster list of things we might have to boycott or rail against? Do we further bury our heads in the evangelical sand, unable to watch Clemens pitch because he has extramarital sex, or Daly hit his nine iron because he drinks too much? Mickey Mantle fooled around on the road and drank too much and he was an icon. Mantle was also downright beautiful at the plate. Ditto for star athletes/playboys Namath behind center and Wilt in the paint.

As we've seen so many times before, boycotting doesn't work. We'll miss watching sports, and the sports machine will keep rolling. Each year there are angry letters to *Sports Illustrated* over the swimsuit issue, and each year there is another swimsuit issue. In fact, the angry letters have almost become part of the enduring ethos of the magazine. But how do we, as Christ followers, maintain, or begin to have, a Philippians 4:8 perspective on sports while still enjoying sports? How do we think about those things that are true, noble, right, and pure? By recognizing those elements can and do exist in sports.

1. ***Truth.*** There *is* absolute truth in sports. Each game has a winner and a loser. Statistics show us that Michael Jordan was a better player than Sam Bowie. Peyton Manning has thrown for more touchdowns than Kyle Orton. These things are all true. Yet plenty of untruth and half-truth remain in sports: Players lie under oath about their involvement in steroid scandals; players commit to and then de-commit from schools; coaches take their dream jobs only to leave a couple years later; etc. We need to pray for discernment in what we're seeing, and help our kids to be discerning as well. Gone are the days of Mickey Mantle, the lantern-jawed, down-home, all-American stud endorsing Ovaltine and hitting home runs while keeping his checkered private life largely private.

2. ***Nobility.*** There *is* nobility in sports. There are herculean, self-sacrificing efforts like former Marshall quarterback Byron Leftwich being carried down the field by his teammates, refusing to come out of the game after breaking his ankle. And there is off-the-field nobility, like the case of former Chiefs running back

Joe Delaney (circa early 1980s) who gave his own life to attempt to save the lives of several drowning children in a Monroe, Louisiana pond.

3. *Rightness.* Sara Tucholsky, a softball player at Western Oregon University, had never before hit a home run, but with two runners on and a strike against her, she did just that, uncorking a shot that cleared the fence against Central Washington University in a 2008 playoff game. Realizing she had missed first base, she planted her right leg to turn around and collapsed with a knee injury. If her teammates helped her around the bases, the home run would be called off. If a pinch runner was called in, the homer would only count as a single. Central Washington first baseman Mallory Holtman, the career home run leader in the Great Northwest Athletic Conference, asked the umpire if *she* could help Tucholsky. The umpire said there was no rule against it, so Holtman and a teammate carried Tucholsky around the field, helping her to touch each bag with her good leg, rendering the home run good, and allowing Western Oregon to advance in the playoffs. Afterward, Holtman said, "In the end, it is not about winning and losing so much. It was about this girl. She hit it over the fence and was in pain, and she deserved a home run."

4. *Purity.* Bleacher seats with your dad at a MLB stadium. Kids playing sports in a vacant lot, with no parental or coach involvement. Division III football. Youth soccer in Eastern Europe. Pond hockey. There are pure aspects awaiting fans at sporting events. In 2007 Jonathan Vaughters, Tour De France veteran and former teammate of Lance Armstrong, helped found a team currently known as Garmin-Slipstream. The team is significant not for its victories—though it has been increasingly competitive on

the international scene—but for the fact that it has committed, as a team, to race clean. Team riders are frequently tested and interviewed regarded potential drug use, and are not permitted to ride if blood tests indicate any possibility of doping. These riders are united in their concern for the health of bicycling as a sport, and cyclists as individuals—and they are willing to sacrifice individual results to clean up the sport.

For all my supposed grousing about the NFL Scouting Combine, I watched nearly all of its coverage this year (2008). I watched Michigan tackle Jake Long run 5.1 seconds in the 40, which is blisteringly fast for a man who weighs 320 pounds. I watched Chris Johnson, a running back from East Carolina, run a 4.2, which is blisteringly fast for anyone in the world. I listened to Rich Eisen banter endlessly with Mike Mayock, who is doing his very best to become the next Mel Kiper. I exposed myself to countless Viagra and huge-truck commercials, while at the same time watching men who I'll never be as big, fast, strong, or ripped as do things that I'll never be able to do. I learned how to size up other human beings, and talk about them like commodities, just like the pros do. I learned that 4.8 seconds in the 40 isn't fast enough for a linebacker, but I already knew that because I ran 4.9 when I played and it wasn't fast enough then either.

I saw all-everything Michigan wide receiver Mario Manningham run a very pedestrian 4.7 seconds in the dash. The announcers talked about him in hushed tones, as though his life were indeed over, or as though he had just lost his entire family in a tragic automobile accident. His 40-yard time was a tragedy of epic combine proportions. How would young Manningham put his life back on track when there were defensive ends like Chris Long who ran faster? Manningham, for the record, would recover and become a third round pick of the New York

Giants. His recovery is nothing short of a triumph of a team that looks beyond the stats to the player's overall talent. Whether it was Mario's sharp pass routes, college production, and/or sure hands, the Giants liked what they saw.

The grass withers, and the flower fades (though it fades much more slowly with Miller High Life, we're told). Today's studs are tomorrow's forgotten heroes. My hope for these athletes, and for myself, is that they find happiness and holiness in Jesus, whether their lives continue on an upward arc or, horror of horrors, they run a tenth of a second slow at the combine.

And sports and sexuality will always be with us, though I'm guessing it all stems from the greater question of where we find our identity. If God didn't create the universe, and we're doing nothing more here than "getting ours" and taking up space, then yes, be very depressed that you aren't 264 pounds of rock-hard muscle with 3 percent body fat. Be jealous and feel cheated that you aren't able to maintain an erection lasting longer than twelve hours.

But if you believe God's truth, declared in the Bible, know this: We're here to bring honor and glory to our Lord. If you're one of the lucky ones who can do that by running fast, congratulations—and enjoy it as the fleeting blessing that it is. And if not—and most of us are not so blessed when it comes to world-class athletic talent—enjoy the gifts the Creator has given you, and use them to bring Him honor.

NOTE

1. I would think the sheer fact that a man would have to watch and, at times, discuss *The View* would be enough to preclude that man from having a relationship with Star Jones.

11

SPORTS *and*
HUMILITY

WHY I LOVE MUHAMMAD ALI
(BUT WHY HE ALSO MAY HAVE RUINED SPORTS)

At home I am a nice guy: but I don't want the world to know.
Humble people, I've found, don't get very far.

MUHAMMAD ALI
(London) *Sunday Express*, January 13, 1963

I am the greatest." With these four words Muhammad Ali (then Cassius Clay)[1] probably did more to renew the public's interest in boxing, and spark the public's interest in Muhammad Ali, than perhaps any other thing he did in his much-written-about career. That phrase, and other Ali-isms, has been used to sell sneakers, to improve our collective self-esteem, and, most practically, to sell boxing tickets during Ali's career. People wanted to see "The Greatest"—either to see him beat up on some poor chump, or to get beat up himself.

Of course, I know that writing an essay critiquing Muhammad Ali is, for some, akin to heresy. I might as well title this chapter, "Why Ted Kluck Is a Hard-hearted Villain."

I saw Muhammad Ali in person at the last professional fight I covered, the Mike Tyson vs. Kevin McBride tilt in Washington, D.C.

(detailed in chapter 3). Ali was stooped over at the waist and shuffled along the floor in slow, deliberate steps. His hair was gray, and he was wearing a floral-print Hawaiian shirt. In the throes of Parkinson's disease, Ali couldn't speak and had to be led into the arena by handlers. At the moment, the tens of thousands or so fans who had gathered to watch Mike Tyson destroy McBride (he wouldn't) were watching a preliminary fight. Upon seeing Ali, the crowd began to chant his name. Before long, even the fighters in the ring seemed to be straining to catch a glimpse of perhaps the most beautiful fighter to ever enter the ring. The crowd chanted for several minutes, while Ali raised a hand in acknowledgment. He was on hand to watch his daughter Laila, one of nine children, fight a white girl from Chicago named Erin Toughill, who I learn from the extensive press packet has nine tattoos on her body and once worked as an auto mechanic.[2]

The Laila Ali/Erin Toughill match would go down in boxing history as one of the most brutal women's matches to date. The win gave Ali the World Boxing Council title, and also allowed her to defend her World Boxing Association title. Toughill would leave the ring after three rounds, her not-unattractive face and braided hair much bloodied.

Muhammad Ali shuffled through the postfight press area, and judging by the looks on faces around the room, most of us were unsure as to what to do. There were nods of acknowledgment and some applause, just for being Muhammad Ali, apparently. It was as though, again, we were eulogizing someone who was still alive. Since the early 1990s Ali has been largely unable to communicate as a public figure, thus ensuring that he'll only be remembered for the things he did while in the "prime" of his life and career.[3]

I'll remember Ali for what he did shortly before and after the Mike Tyson/Kevin McBride fight. Before the fight he spent nearly an hour in Mike Tyson's locker room, rubbing Tyson's shoulders and just spending time with him. I know this because there was a camera in the locker room, and I happened to be standing in the MCI Center tunnel watching this footage silently unfold while a prelim fight took place a few feet away in the ring.

After the match, Ali would return again to Tyson's locker room and stay there for a long time, giving encouragement to the former champ. It was a moving moment—two once-proud warriors humbled by their sport, both of whom took savage beatings at the ends of careers that lasted too long.

On a fall afternoon in Detroit in 2007, Lions wide receiver Roy Williams catches a routine eight-yard hitch and is tackled shortly thereafter. After popping up off the turf, he gives his trademark "first down" dance, which involves a forward lunge accompanied by a flourish of his right hand that mimics the signal a ref gives when he indicates a first down. This is significant only because Williams's team is down by three touchdowns. Williams addresses detractors after the game who criticized his need to do the first-down dance with his team down by such a margin by explaining, "I'm an entertainer."

On the same fall afternoon, Baltimore Ravens veteran linebacker and future Hall of Famer Ray Lewis is introduced at M&T Bank Stadium[4] and gyrates out of the tunnel, flapping his arms and screaming demonically at the top of his lungs. This dance, which has also become something of a trademark, serves the dual purpose of whipping the Baltimore crowd and his teammates into a white-hot frenzy. He wears a gang-style do-rag on his head, and both of his arms are covered in tattoos. For the record, Lewis was acquitted of the knife murder of another man several years ago, and was later lauded for his Christian faith in *Sports Illustrated* where he appeared on the cover under the heading "God's Linebacker."

A year later, in the formerly Katrina-ravaged city of New Orleans, *Sports Spectrum* magazine[5] cover boy and current Orlando Magic boy wonder Dwight Howard is preparing for his next-to-last dunk in the NBA All-Star Sprite Slam Dunk Contest.[6] Howard is only twenty-two but has been in the league since forgoing college basketball to be selected first overall in the 2004 draft. Howard is 6 foot 11 and 265 pounds, boasting a forty-inch vertical leap—unbelievably rare in a guy his size. Upon his graduation from Southwest Christian Academy in Atlanta, Howard, at eighteen, expressed a desire to be a light for Christ in the NBA. In 2007 he had a child out of wedlock with a former Magic dancer.

This is a good place to come clean with the fact that I have become really cynical about these Christian-athlete types. Believe me when I say that I mean no ill will to Howard, and don't mean to single him out as an example of the Christian-athlete-makes-a-very-public-mistake phenomenon. We've all sinned and fallen short of the glory of God (Romans 3:23).

THE BRIGHT LIGHTS

But back to Howard and the 2008 Sprite Slam Dunk Contest. The crowd is buzzing with anticipation, and the room has the NBA requisite random-celebrities-meets-hip-hop-event vibe. Arnold Schwarzenegger sports an embalmed, politician's smile on the front row. Spike Lee occupies a seat nearby. Magic Johnson is at the celebrity judges' table, and the rest of the dunkers—mostly NBA no-names like Jamario Moon, Gerald Green, and Rudy Gay—wait expectantly to see not if they will lose this contest but rather how.

The lights are bright in the arena, and Howard is walking around with a one-hundred-watt smile on his face. Finally, he removes his jersey to reveal a blue, Superman spandex shirt underneath. A teammate helps him affix a red Superman cape on his back to complete the ensemble. The crowd and the celebrity judges go berserk, as though this is the most singularly creative flourish they have ever seen in the history of the once-Gatorade, now-Sprite Slam Dunk Contest.

I'm of the opinion that the dunk contest is the highlight of the NBA calendar. While NBA games often seem *Groundhog Day*-esque[7] in that there are eighty-two of them and they usually feature two guys playing isolation ball while the other eight stand around, the dunk contest provides a great venue for the NBA's superior athletes to display their grace, beauty, and superior athleticism. It has also provided some singular NBA moments, including 5 foot 6 Spud Webb's improbable victory over Dominique Wilkins, and Michael Jordan soaring through the air from the free throw line.

So here is Howard, in full Superman regalia, pumping the crowd into a frenzy before his dunk. You quickly realize that the dunk contest is about 90 percent posturing, self-promoting, pomp and circumstance, and only about 10 percent actual dunking. The time in between dunks seems to never end. Finally, Howard high points the basketball after a bounce and throws it downward through the hoop (that's how high he is) as the crowd goes wild and his Superman cape trails behind him. He then gestures to the crowd and soaks up their adulation for a number of minutes while the celebrity judges howl, exchange high-fives, and raise their "10" cards, because that (howling, high-fiving) is what celebrity judges do.

NBA types are crediting that dunk and its accompanying excitement with "restoring the public's interest" in the NBA Slam Dunk Contest. But I think it probably has more to do with the presence of an actual star (Howard) on the roster of dunkers. Shortly after Jordan decided he was done dunking, the crown was won by a list of also-rans that includes Kenny "Sky" Walker, Dee Brown (Reebok Pumps and blindfold), Cedric Ceballos, Harold Miner (said to be the next Michael

Jordan), and Brent Barry (one of Rick Barry's kids, notable for being a white guy).

So what does Muhammad Ali have to do with Roy Williams, Ray Lewis, and the NBA Dunk Contest? I think everything. We've become a sports culture of self-glorifiers, and Christian athletes certainly aren't immune to it. Because Ali set the table for chest-thumping swagger with "I am the greatest" and his other hubristic flourishes, we've been left with a sports landscape littered with little counterfeit Alis who happen to possess none of the charisma of the original.

Here are some reasons the Ali gimmick "worked" and the present-day show by others (Howard, Lewis, Williams, etc.) doesn't:

1. *Ali was first.* Prior to Muhammad Ali, sports were generally team-oriented and boxers were predictable. Ali was the first fighter, at least on a wide, public scale, to provide a decent interview, and he soon learned that cutting an effective promo would have a very positive effect on his ticket sales and, therefore, his bottom line.

2. *Ali was an unbelievable athlete.* Ali also said, "It's not bragging if you back it up." He's half right. It's still bragging and it's still obnoxious. And, probably, fully half of the American sports-fan public hated Ali in his era. But they still watched him, admitting that he was a beautifully effective fighter in his prime. And they bought tickets because they really loved the idea of Joe Frazier knocking his block off. Ali knew this and used it to his advantage (see: ticket sales).

3. *Ali was the only one, at the time, doing his schtick.* Nowadays, after every special teams tackle, there is a third-string linebacker running out of the pile, ripping his helmet off, and beating his

chest. That linebacker likes the idea of seeing his mug on television, and he thinks that by pounding his chest and dancing around he is somehow helping to get noticed and increase his marketability. Unfortunately, everybody is doing this now, which makes most games really hard to watch and renders all of these guys just as nameless and faceless as they normally are. It's just that now they're nameless, faceless guys dancing around instead of nameless, faceless guys walking back to the huddle.

4. *Ali got credit for some things that, in retrospect, he probably shouldn't have gotten credit for.* By not wanting to go to Vietnam—a war many Americans thought we shouldn't be in anyway—Ali became something of a voice for anti-war America, and has continued to be a voice for other positive things in a feel-good, soft-focus, "remember-when" type of way.

5. *Ali did his thing in an individual sport.* Ali made boxing relevant, as boxing is only relevant when it has a charismatic star. Unfortunately, many athletes in team sports adopted the Ali ethic to less than inspiring results.

6. *Ali was unusually gifted and full of charisma.* Ali was attractive to look at—a fact he reminded people of often. He was also an incredibly gifted communicator with the ability to captivate a variety of audiences. He found allies who could help him rather easily (Howard Cosell) and even his adversaries (Frazier, Foreman, everybody else) were aware that his schtick was ultimately going to increase their bottom lines.

A CULTURE OF
RAMPANT SELF-EXPRESSION

Those six things, I think, made the Ali gimmick work, where today's athletes fall short. Much of this (chest-thumping, self-glorification, me-first), I think, we can blame on Ali. We can also probably blame him for the culture of rampant self-expression that has seeped into professional sports. A reporter's dream, Ali filled notebooks for decades with quotes, poems, and brashness that spanned a spectrum from banal and stupid to downright insightful. Now, current athletes like Terrell Owens and Chad Johnson feel that they need to be "entertaining" or "shocking" each time they open their mouths, and unfortunately it just sounds like so much noise. Also unfortunate is the fact that at least for elite athletes like these, it still "works" in the sense that these athletes are still on television more often than Marvin Harrison (Colts), who is every bit as good.

Am I a curmudgeon for not liking self-expression? Maybe. I'm expressing myself in this book, so perhaps I'm a walking contradiction. But I also think there's a time and a place for self-expression, and perhaps catching a six-yard hitch in the fourth quarter of a meaningless game isn't that time or place.

In general, I don't think most sports fans want their athletes to be entertainers. We have real entertainers for that. I think what many people want to see, when watching sports, is people who are incredibly gifted at a sport and are also incredibly competitive. These are traits that made Muhammad Ali and Michael Jordan impossible to ignore. But now that many athletes are expressing themselves on a nonstop basis, it's easy to wish they wouldn't. Athletes have gotten a little more cartoonish. And a lot less humble.

God opposes the proud but gives grace to the humble.
James 4:6 (see Proverbs 3:34)

So what does any of this matter, and what's the endgame here? I'm not sure, except that nowhere in the Bible does anyone advocate self-promotion. Indeed the Bible is full of thoughts and parables that directly contradict this ethic. The last shall be first and the first shall be last. Jesus washing the feet of the disciples. Meekness, kindness, and humility are lauded as fruits of the spirit.[8] Nowhere in the Bible does anyone say "be brash, controversial, and self-glorifying as long as it helps you sell tickets and secure endorsement deals."

And as J. C. Ryle wrote in his classic *Holiness*, "Thousands have trodden the path you are pursuing, and have awoke too late to find it end in misery and eternal ruin. They have fought hard for wealth, and honor, and office, and promotion, and turned their backs on God, and Christ, and heaven, and the world to come. And what has their end been? Often, far too often, they have found out that their whole life has been a grand mistake. They have tasted by bitter experience the feelings of the dying statesman who cried aloud in his last hours, 'The battle is fought: but the victory is not won.'"[9]

If we're to live out our biblical Christianity as athletes and fans, we're called to a higher standard than the one set by the marketplace. Our set-apartness should bleed into the arena just as it does (hopefully) in the office for those of us who aren't paid to play.

So maybe instead of thumping our chests and pointing at the sky to "be a light" in the football community, the Christian athlete simply walks back to the huddle. Maybe instead of soaking up the adulation of an unbelievable dunk, he just goes back and sits on the bench afterward. Maybe instead of kneeling in the end zone for an elaborate show of prayer, he just flips the ball to the ref and thanks God on his own for life, health, and the ability to play a fun game for money. Perhaps he does so, praying that God will give him grace, and striving after true humility to echo Proverbs 3:34.

And in doing so, he might just shock the world.

NOTES

1. Cassius Clay first made the boast in 1963 before facing Sonny Liston, repeated after his upset win over Liston on February 26, 1964. On February 7, 1965, Clay converted to Islam and took the name Muhammad Ali (see www.historyorb.com/religion/Islam). Three months later Ali met Liston in a rematch and scored a first round knockout.

2. These two facts, alone, both made me feel a little bit less masculine than Toughill—coupled with the fact that she is also a professional boxer. While her career as a boxer was marginal, she's currently ranked number one in her weight division as an MMA (mixed martial arts) fighter.

3. Few people, thankfully, remember the beatings he took at the end of his career at the hands of fighters like Trevor Berbick and Larry Holmes.

4. Whose name is not quite as cozy as US Cellular Field in Chicago, home of the White Sox, or the TD Banknorth Garden in Boston, which used to be known as the Boston Garden. I hate corporate naming.

5. This is a sports magazine that's been around for a while and is known for doing mostly formulaic, PR-friendly features on Christian athletes who often talk about how excited they are to use their pro-ness as a tool for sharing faith. For the record, I cowrite a column in the magazine and have done so for several years. I also like the magazine and think it's good.

6. Slogan: They dunk, you decide. This means that fans can watch the dunks and then text their "votes" via a number flashed on the screen during the contest. This does make me wonder about the significance of the "Celebrity Judges" at courtside, including Magic Johnson and Clyde "The Glide" Drexler, though they may just be there for decoration and entertainment as per Simon Cowell, Randy Jackson, and Paula Abdul in the final rounds of *American Idol*.

7. Meaning endlessly repetitive, in the way that the movie portrayed the Bill Murray character waking up and doing the same thing every day. Also, almost everybody makes the playoffs in the NBA, which further renders the regular season kind of pointless. Also, the playoffs last forever.

8. See Matthew 20:16; John 13:1–17; and Galatians 5:22–23, respectively.

9. J. C. Ryle, *Holiness* (Peabody, Mass.: HendricksonPublishers, 2007), 81.

12

BLACK
LIKE ME

Teamwork is what the Green Bay Packers were all about.
They didn't do it for individual glory.
They did it because they loved one another.

VINCE LOMBARDI
Head Coach, Green Bay Packers

I t's one in the morning. I'm on a bus, surrounded by large black men, many of whom have tattoos. There is a variety of cheap, domestic light beers being passed around, and a couple of flasks of hard liquor. They're large men, and they stare vacantly out the windows. Some try to sleep. There is the faint din of hip-hop music pulsing out of iPods. Some laughter in the back. The streetlights flicker occasionally, and I'm reminded by my reflection in the glass that mine is one of the only white faces on the bus. I can see bags under my eyes. I can see two days' worth of stubble. I don't like the way I look, and I don't especially like the way anyone else on the bus looks either. This is par for the course, I think, in bus travel. Beautiful people don't travel this way.

The bus rumbles to a stop in front of a bar in Ann Arbor, Michigan. A few groans can be heard, but the majority of us step over legs and luggage and amble off the bus and into the bar.

During the bus ride I overhead a couple of random conversations that had either spiritual or social value:

- A discussion about how hard it is to be a parent, with a guy named L. J. who is raising two daughters by himself.
- A conversation on the merits of health/wealth/prosperity tele-vangelist T. D. Jakes, which led into a subconversation on materialism that is especially ironic, given the fact that we're all eating food that came from gas stations.

If this were a Greyhound bus, and I were traveling on it, say, from Detroit to Anywhere, USA, I would probably feel profoundly nervous about the above scenario. I don't consider myself a racist, but I'm just saying, I'd be nervous, being in the minority. That probably makes me a horrible person. But this is a busload of my teammates, also my friends, whiling away hours in the iron lung. Granted, most of my teammates (black and white) are singularly focused on how much beer they could consume before getting home. Some are concerned with finding female companionship for the evening—and not in the Proverbs 31 sense.

THE MOST SEGREGATED—AND INTEGRATED—TIME SLOTS IN AMERICA

During the trip, I'm reminded of the oft-quoted fact about "Sunday morning being the most segregated time slot in American culture." This is always tossed out as a way to cleverly chide the church for somehow being unconcerned with worshiping alongside those of other races. For the record, I don't think this is especially true (the part about the church being unconcerned). I think churches are more diverse than we give them credit for. But as a very smart pastor friend of mine from a predominantly black community once pointed out: People go where they like it. It is what it is.

And if 9 a.m. to noon is the most segregated time slot in America, 1 p.m. to 4 p.m. (the early game) and 4 p.m. to 8 p.m. (the late game) may be the most integrated. This isn't a plea for churches to run out and start sports ministries, but it's more of an admission of what those of us in sports already know: Athletes are good at race relations because they aren't trying to be good at race relations.

That said, give or take a couple of guys, the entirety of my African-American friends are represented on this bus, which we now reboard. I've spent more time with these guys over the past several months than any of my white friends at church, or even the majority of my family members. So much so that I'm beginning to speak like my teammates.

I've found out all that we have in common as black and white players, namely, that none of us is being paid by our owner, who in the time-honored tradition of minor league ownership has run out of money and completely flaked out. And we all have injuries—we're all hurting in one place or another, from the rigors of a long season with too much contact, not enough padding under the AstroTurf, and not enough medical care. L. J.'s knee is shot. Azriel ripped off a toenail in the game tonight. My shoulder is throbbing both from the pounding it's taken on the field and the twelve hours of jostling against the wall of a bus. We're all, also, in some state of being broke. Playing minor league football is, fiscally, really stupid. I don't recommend it. We all have families and relationships that we don't always understand. Most of us miss wives, girlfriends, and kids.

What's also true is that I really like these guys, and I know I'll miss them now that the season of Saturday night lights is ending.

A few years later, except for L. J., the linebacker with the daughters, I haven't really kept in touch with any of them. I've retreated back to my white suburban church, and my white suburban friends who have great dinner parties and interesting conversations about things like Calvinism, whether there will be actual crowns in heaven, and how hard it is to homeschool their kids. There's nothing wrong with these conversations, and I'm not even especially stressed out over the fact that there's not much diversity in our church.

But what I'm concerned about is the fact that the only place I've ever felt at home with black folks has been in a locker room, on a team bus, in a boxing gym, or on the field.

I have several friends who have gone through a masters-level program in social work at a large Big Ten University, and most of them have come out completely disillusioned with the church. Encouraged no doubt by Geoge Barna's *Revolution*, or by any number of emergent authors, they chuck their "traditional" church experience in search of a more "diverse" body, as diversity has, for them, eclipsed doctrine, worship, and fellowship on the chain of church importance.

What they're looking for, of course, doesn't exist: a church with teaching and fellowship that is stimulating enough to suit their advanced-degreed intellect, free-trade organic coffee and programs nuanced enough to suit their suburban tastes, and a church with enough "diversity" to suit their newfound passion for wanting to worship alongside people who don't look like they do. These, for the record, are all good things. What they're not ready to do, though, is go and "be" the diversity at a predominantly black church. They're not ready to give up a nursery where they get a pager in return and feel completely comfortable leaving their kids. They're not ready to face the parking issue in the rough neighborhood. Nor are they ready to forgo coffee in the lobby and mingle with a roomful of people who look, talk, dress, and act differently than they do. They want comfort. And that street runs both ways. People go where they like it. It is what it is.

There have, of course, been whole books written on this topic—not sports and race, but race and the church. In *The Church Enslaved: A Spir-*

ituality for Racial Reconciliation, by Tony Campolo and Michael Battle, the authors believe that American churches need to do more to overcome America's legacy of racial discrimination, which also means overcoming the not small problems of current racial discrimination and neglect within the churches. The authors blame Western individualism for many of the church's failures in connecting racially, citing individualism and even the notion of "a personal relationship with Christ" for all manner of "in and out" and "us and them" dynamics.

But as anyone who has ever played organized sports can attest, sports is probably the second-least individualistic activity on earth, next to military service. Anyone who's ever played for an "old school" coach knows that their old school-ness is wrapped up in communicating to you, at least for a time, that you are not special, and that your unique inner workings and felt needs don't matter nearly as much as the needs of the team. It's the subjugation of self for the greater good. Athletes, black and white, understand this dynamic intuitively.

Interestingly, though, sports has its own radical distinctions: winner and loser, starter and backup, highly paid star and league-minimum role player, coach and player, player and fan. I'm not suggesting that sports is a neatly packaged egalitarian society where everyone is on equal footing, I'm only suggesting that this is a realistic part of sports.

Azriel Woodson, from the bus ride I described above, is black, a linebacker, and a minister. He's also a better player than me. He's a starter and I'm a backup, and he in fact beats me down in drills with startling regularity. He has left me bruised and bloodied on more than one occasion. This inequality doesn't prevent us from being friends and brothers in Christ. Azriel is interested in spiritual things. He is trying to make wise choices, and was one of the few who didn't get up and amble into the bar in Ann Arbor that night. We are "being the church" together outside the walls of church.

That's not to say that things are perfect, racially, in sports. In 2005,

Air Force Academy head football coach (and Christian) Fisher DeBerry, blamed a loss to Texas Christian University on the fact that TCU had "more black players" who "ran faster." DeBerry, guilty of speaking what athletes white and black have known for decades and even snickered about together in private, was publicly castigated and made to make yet another halfhearted sports apology (see chapter 1 regarding sports apologies). DeBerry's gaffe is the kind of thing that keeps university administrators and professors up at night. He was doofus enough to publicly say what those same administrators and professors see each Saturday from their skyboxes (admins) and box seats (profs): Speed wins football games, and, for reasons I'm not intelligent enough to know or even comment on, black players have speed. DeBerry's only indiscretion, as stated by National Public Radio's Frank DeFord, was being dumb enough not to know how to say what he said without really saying it so literally.

See also Al Campanis of the Los Angeles Dodgers, who explained in a televised interview with *Nightline*'s Ted Koppell that "I truly believe they (blacks) may not have some of the necessities to be a field manager or perhaps a general manager." Campanis was fired within forty-eight hours, never to be heard from again, and his theory has been roundly disproved by successful black GMs and coaches and GMs like football's Jerry Reese, Tony Dungy, and Lovie Smith, and baseball's Tony Reagins, Kenny Williams, Dusty Baker, and Jerry Manuel.

LEARNING TO GET ALONG IN SPORTS

This is a point of great consternation for everyone, it seems, except the athletes, who year in and year out perform together mostly without racial incident. It is only athletes, black or white, who can refer to each other as "the black guy" or "the white guy" without anyone cringing or without any major PC (politically correct) bells and whistles going off.

There are the race relations you learn in your "Intro to Civil Rights" summer course, and those you learn when you walk into a boxing gym in the seedy part of town, next to the check-cashing joints, the porno shops, and the hubcap places. Every head turns to watch the white boy. How he wraps his hands. How he stands. How he hits the heavy bag. You feel conspicuous. You feel like you'll never fit in. If you're white and in the team minority, it dawns on you, quickly, that this is often how black players feel in a predominately white society. But instead of feeling guilty, you just box, and soon, magically, you're just another guy with a left hook that couldn't crack an egg.

It's been a long night in Battle Creek, Michigan, and we've put a pounding on the visiting New York Revolution in front of the eight hundred or so fans who wandered in or found free tickets. We're up by a tidy margin so the coach puts me in to cover kickoffs. I jog out across the rock-hard Astroturf with my friend L. J.

"Line up next to me, Paperboy."

I see him grinning behind the black bars of our helmets, the whites of his eyes glowing in contrast to his dark face. I'm aware that there are huge differences between us—upbringing, worship style, views on sexuality in relationships, views on politics. But I'm not thinking of any of that stuff, as I settle into my stance next to L. J., the huge number 5 stretched tight across his shoulder pads. His nickname is Superman, he played collegiately at Indiana University, and he's arguably our best athlete.

I'm also not aware that over the next two years we will have many telephone conversations and e-mails about the core tenets of Christianity, and that our friendship will go beyond our shared experiences as black and white football players.

Our kicker puts his toe into the ball and I hurl myself into the most frantic five seconds in sports—the kamikaze-like dash down the field that is called "special teams." My job is to run over, around, or through opposing blockers and get to the ballcarrier, who cradles the ball into his arms at the opposing goal line. He's a black kid himself, with his own dreams of NFL stardom, his own overpriced receiver's gloves, and his own teammates.

I can't hear anything but the sound of L. J. Parker's breathing and my own as we both fly down the field, unhinged, on a night that both of us wish would never end.

A TOWN,
a TORNADO,
and a TEAM

The sounds coming from the practice field are the usual autumn sounds—pads cracking, whistles chirping, and the constant staccato of the sort of insensitive-but-completely-hilarious male banter that is probably only still permissible in our country in football or military settings. In my first year as a defensive line coach, I've grown so fond of this banter that I've already begun to miss it, though our 2008 playoff run—the first for the school since 2002—is just beginning.

The universality of high school football is also what makes it unique. All across the country in the fall, a small number of high school students at schools begin to do things that are completely counterintuitive. They run endless sprints (we call them Green Bays), they don heavy padding, and hit each other for hours on end as Al Gore's global warming sun bakes down upon them. Some are recruited by colleges—

scrutinized within an inch of their life by middle-aged men on the Internet—but most just finish with their memories as seniors. For some, like my defensive tackle Dillon Young, it was proving to himself that he could play varsity football, stepping in and knocking a kid's helmet off against Portland. For others, like our quarterback John Vogl, it's proving to himself that he could run the veer offense.

There are several antidotes, I suppose, for being sick of football. For me, a good place to start seemed like some time away from players Pac Man Jones, Tank Johnson, Mike Vick, coaches Dennis Franchione (and his infamous Texas A&M e-mails), and Nick Saban (and his less-than-forthright denials), and the rest of the television time outs, booth reviews, and general multimillionaire madness that make up professional football. (I include in this "professional" category major college football.) For me, it meant more football, but coaching high school kids instead of covering pros. As an assistant coach, I had a new defense to learn. I had to learn how to handle the veer offense. I soon had discarded practice plans and Gatorade bottles threatening to take over the inside of my truck.

And one Thursday, in October 2007, I watched the weather reports detailing a tornado that ripped through Williamston, Michigan, taking parts of homes, and two lives with it. I thought about our newly renovated stadium, which lost a scoreboard and had its giant metal light poles snapped in half like toothpicks. I wondered if my players were okay, if their houses had power, and privately hoped we wouldn't play on Friday night. We were 7–1, and had already secured our place in the high school playoffs.

Word came on Friday that another school, Okemos High School, offered the use of their stadium, and that our game against Chesaning would indeed happen on Friday night. So we got dressed, got taped,

and boarded a bus, just like normal, but instead of going to our stadium, the bus drove past the fallen trees and the cleanup crews into the
Lansing area's toniest suburb.

Being "salt and light" to a person becomes remarkably simple in
times like this. You put an arm around a kid. You ask how his family is
doing. Our starting guard, Tyler Forbush, lost his grandfather a few
days before the tornado and has been uncharacteristically quiet and
subdued. We're both believers, and communicate a great deal through
a hug, a pat on the helmet, or a glance across the locker room. He knows
I'm praying for him and the presence of each other in this room makes
both of us feel better.

It's our final regular season game, but the kids are scared tonight.
Many of them are woefully sleep-deprived, and the shower they'll take
in the Okemos locker room after the game will be the first they've taken
in a few days. They're unable to conjure even the most artificial of swagger and confidence that usually fills high school locker rooms on game
nights. There's no heavy-metal music. No jumping around. Just scared,
tired kids under green plastic and nylon.

Okemos is home to the Okemos Chieftains, and we dress in their
locker room, under their cheesy motivational posters, and ultimately
get whipped on their field in a driving, cold rainstorm that is essentially the tail end of the line of weather that trashed Williamston. In the
Disney version we would have listened to a stirring speech that didn't
leave a dry eye in the house, and then dedicated the victory to the town.
Instead, we lost. There will be film watched, and then it will be archived
and we'll move on. Football is tidy like that.

Our team, like many others, has the one kid who looks like he's
thirty-five years old. Ours is named Donnie Stiffler and he's a captain,
an all-state shot-putter, and truly a man among boys on the field. Donnie and his senior teammate at linebacker, Spenser Bradley, are the
kind of players that make coaches look good. Donnie and Spenser

would have their senior night, and walk their parents onto the field, in this replacement stadium. It wasn't the way it was supposed to go down, after a great training camp, and an unlikely 7-0 start that included a last-second victory over Portland, an overtime victory over Charlotte, and a conference championship for the first time since the early 1990s. It was supposed to end in a few more thrillers—a few more stadium emptying, field-rushing victories in our house.

The season ended for real the next Friday, on our home field, surrounded by the vestiges of fresh tornado damage—tarps flapped over exposed homes, trees sheared off at the trunk, and our stadium's light poles, snapped like toothpicks, replaced by temporary lighting rigs. We had the opportunity to play the game at the 75,000 seat Spartan Stadium at nearby Michigan State University, but chose instead to play at home.

Our opponent that night was the Belding Redskins, a team from up north with a legendary old coach and an even more antiquated offense (the Wing T) that they run to perfection. The hard-fought playoff game, on an eerily warm night, ended with our team trailing by a point when the gun sounded. Our kids cried, especially the seniors who would probably never play organized football again. It was weird to see big, strong, cocky high school kids, who spend most of their time driving Camaros and flirting with girls, crying. Once football is over, it's over. I remembered how I cried after my last high school game, and apologized to my coach for not doing more. This scenario is played out in every town across the United States at the end of every fall and will until the end of time.

This strikes me as why we play, and why we buy tickets to cheer the people who play. We live for these moments—the hard-fought close games where there is relentless combat, but where the combatants clearly respect, and even enjoy, each other. This still happens at the major college and professional level, and the hope and expectation of that happening is what keeps us coming back. As players we hold ourselves—our attitudes, our bravery, and our statistics—up to the light of those who have gone before us, and as fans we wonder how we would react or perform in similar situations. We hold ourselves up to the light of their performances. I thank God for sports, for this reason and many others.

But I also remembered our pregame prayer that night. We gathered around, like we always do, and knelt down on the concrete around our head coach, Steve Kersten, who loves the Lord. I prayed in my head like I always do, for a safe, injury-free game for our players and theirs. And Steve thanked God for the kids, for the fun we'd had together, and for the privilege of being young, healthy athletes about to play a great game under the lights on Friday night.

ACKNOWLEDGMENTS

ome of my fondest memories of childhood are of long car rides, coming back at night in dark cars illuminated by highway lights, after going to see the Fort Wayne Komets play hockey or the Indianapolis Colts play football. These were one-on-one times with my dad, and the conversations were (and still are) tremendous. We would sometimes talk about what we'd seen, but would often end up talking about other things—some sports related, some not. I'd like to thank my dad for talking about sports and life with me. We talked while we were driving to and from sporting events, we talked while watching sporting events, and we talked while training for sporting events. It occurs to me that much of my spiritual formation took place during these talks. My dad probably read a grand total of zero books about parenting when

I was a kid, but he was great at driving, talking, and being available. For this I am eternally grateful.

To Madison, Andy, and the rest of the folks at Moody Publishers for being loyal, generous, and great to work with in general. It's fun to write books with you guys.

I'd like to thank Mike Tyson, Ricky Williams, Tony Mandarich, and the rest of the guys I wrote about in this book for being interesting, and for not being afraid to be honest about your failures as well as your successes. The world of sports is better for your existence in it. My hope and prayer for the three of you, in particular, would be that you would come to a saving knowledge of Jesus Christ.

My writing career is better for the existence of Andrew Wolgemuth, my agent in some small part because it gives me the chance to say things like "my agent." And my life is better for the existence of my wife, Kristin, and my sons, Tristan and Maxim, who I look forward to sharing sports with as they grow older.

SEX, SUSHI, & SALVATION

Jumping from adventure to adventure, Christian George takes the reader from a fear of life's turbulent experiences to a confidence that comes from knowing God. Through seemingly random but progressively connected stories, the three deepest hungers of the human heart are unearthed:

> the drive for intimacy,
>> the comfort of community,
>>> and the expectation of eternity.

THE MESSAGE BEHIND
THE MOVIE

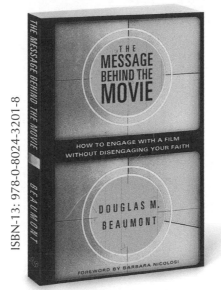

ISBN-13: 978-0-8024-3201-8

Christian books on movies often expose Hollywood's messages without teaching what to do about them or how to turn those messages into opportunities for sharing the gospel. In contrast, with this book readers will be able to understand the basics of movie interpretation, identify and interpret key ideas, and provide an uncomplicated defense of the Christian worldview. In a fun and approachable style, apologetics professor and lover of movies Douglas Beaumont enables all of us to wisely engage with a film—to engage our culture **without** disengaging from our faith!

1-800-678-8812 • MOODYPUBLISHERS.COM